MODEL RAILWAY DETAILING
MANUAL

1. On the LNWR main line west of **Coventry**, LMS Class 5MT 4-6-0 No. 45276 heads a short parcels train on a murky winter's morning in 1962. The scene is brought to life by an LMS signal bracket guarding the junction to Nuneaton. The grassy cutting is further enhanced by trees in the background, the telegraph and a slender lattice footbridge. Such a scene today is likely to be obscured by uncut trees and undergrowth. Note the four support guys and a top bracing rod on this tall bracket.

MODEL RAILWAY DETAILING MANUAL

A SOURCE BOOK OF PERIOD PHOTOGRAPHS FROM THE STEAM AGE

ALAN POSTLETHWAITE

Haynes Publishing

© Alan Postlethwaite 2005

All rights reserved. No part of this publication may be reproduced, stored in a retrieval system or transmitted, in any form or by any means, electronic, mechanical, photocopying, recording or otherwise, without prior permission in writing from the publisher.

First published in 2005

A catalogue record for this book is available from the British Library

ISBN 1 84425 201 9

Library of Congress catalog card no: 2004117159

Published by Haynes Publishing, Sparkford,
Yeovil, Somerset BA22 7JJ, UK

Tel: 01963 442030 Fax: 01963 440001
Int. tel: +44 1963 442030 Int. fax: +44 1963 440001
E-mail: sales@haynes.co.uk
Website: www.haynes.co.uk

Haynes North America, Inc.,
861 Lawrence Drive, Newbury Park,
California 91320, USA

Printed and bound in England by J. H. Haynes & Co. Ltd, Sparkford

While every effort is taken to ensure the accuracy of the information given in this book, no liability can be accepted by the author or publishers for any loss, damage or injury caused by errors in, or omissions from, the information given.

Front cover: Built by Ken Ross in OO gauge, *Corrinford* is one of some eight layouts of the Phoenix Model Railway Club at Quedgeley Enterprise Park, Gloucester. This GWR branch terminus is a good example of getting the amount of detail 'just right', leaving no space neglected but not cramming in too many buildings, people or other accessories.

Contents

	Plate Nos
Introduction	1–4

Station buildings
Station approaches	5–8
Grand frontages	9–12
Stone, brick and tiles	13–16
Multi-storey buildings	17–20
Booking offices	21–24

Platform browsing
Busy platforms	25–28
Urban platforms	29–32
Salient canopies	33–36
Integral canopies	37–40
Open footbridges	41–44
Covered footbridges	45–48
Platform shelters	49–53
Platform lamps	54–57
Botanic platforms	58–61
Station signs	62–67

Station layouts
Branch termini	68–71
Country stations	72–75
Complete halts	76–79
Station trackwork	80–84
Closed stations	85–89

Parcels and freight
Platform barrows	90–93
Parcels and mails	94–98
Goods shed layouts	99–102
Goods stations	103–106
Loading the goods	107–110
Marshalling yards	111–114

Train perspectives
Shifting coal	115–118
Heavy freight	119–122
Distant steam	123–126
Stopping trains	127–130
Trains under trees	131–134
Little trains	135–139
Transient diesels	140–143
Steam doubles	144–147

Along the line
Urban backdrops	148–152
Lineside industries	153–156
Riverside settings	157–160
Steel bridges	161–164
Brick bridges	165–168
Tunnel approaches	169–172
Cutting angles	173–176
Embankments	177–180
Cast-iron signs	181–187
Point levers	188–191
Level crossings	192–195
The telegraph	196–199
Lineside huts	200–204
Jungle encroachment	205–208
Surprise encounters	209–213

Signals
Wooden signal posts	214–218
Rail-built and lattice posts	219–224
Tubular signal posts	225–228
Signal brackets	229–234
Stretched signalry	235–239

Signal boxes
Low platform boxes	240–243
Timber signal boxes	244–247
Brick-to-floor boxes	248–252
Brick-to-roof boxes	253–256
Stone-and-brick boxes	257–261
Signal box mechanisms	262–265
Signal box variations	266–269

Rolling stock
Re-used coaches	270–275
Passenger brakes	276–279
Lonesome wagons	280–284
Grounded bodies	285–289

Locomotive facilities
Small MPDs	290–293
Large MPDs	294–298
Steam servicing	299–302
Water columns	303–306
Water towers	307–312

Abbreviations	–
References	–
Index	313

2. The platform ends at **Liverpool Street** are not covered by the overall roof but this long platform has its own canopy. In 1959, smoke and railway enthusiasts circulate as two trains prepare to depart. Centre-stage is GER N7 class 0-6-2T No. 69614 – always spotlessly clean as the station pilot. It heads an RCTS railtour through London and North Kent. Beyond, BR 'Britannia' class Pacific No. 70003 *John Bunyan* heads an East Anglian express. Note the modernistic electric lamps and standards, also the assortment of barrows.

Introduction

Railway modelling has three main facets – technical, geo-historical and aesthetic. The technical facet is concerned with finding and adapting a suitable railway room, building baseboards, designing a layout, laying the track, electrifying it and maintaining it all. The geo-historical facet is concerned with choosing the era, geography and railway companies to be modelled and then researching the designs and liveries of the respective trains, stations and ancillary items.

Aesthetics is about adding the trains, buildings, scenery and ancillaries to make the railway look finished, authentic and 'come alive'. At this stage, a few touches of intuitive genius can transform a technical toy into a work of art. This cannot be taught or defined; you can only study the layout and experiment with different ideas until you get the setting 'just right'. One common mistake is to add too many ancillary items in a small space. Ken Ross's *Corrinford* (on the cover) is a good example of getting the amount of detail 'just right'.

Standards of modelling vary from fine (every rivet counted) to coarse (off-the-shelf toys), the latter often producing an 'impressionist' finish which is nevertheless satisfying. A model railway can take anything from a few months to a lifetime to complete. The best results achieve a balance between the three main facets and are sufficiently robust and reliable to be exhibited. Given the right temperament, this can be achieved both by groups and by individuals. The final test is always whether or not visitors are captivated.

This manual is intended to assist aspiring modellers in the geo-historical and aesthetic facets of modelling in the British steam era. The pictures are concerned mainly with detail and include the overall impression of a railway in urban and rural settings. All the photographs were taken by the author between 1958 and 1967, covering five BR Regions plus the Isle of Man. The age of the subject matter varies from the pre-Grouping era, when a hundred or so companies, great and small, competed for dominance and survival, through the golden years of the Big Four (1923-47) to BR (1948 on).

The term 'Steam Age' encompasses much more than steam locomotives. It includes all the assets found in stations, yards and along the lines – old assets that were commonplace until the BR Modernisation Plan took hold during the 1950s and '60s. It is remarkable, for example, that so many lovely Victorian signal boxes survived into BR days, together with Edwardian wooden rolling stock and signalling systems from the inter-war years. The origins and features of such artefacts are identified to assist in any year of modelling from about 1900 until the mid-1960s. The liveries may have changed as the railways were grouped and nationalised, but the basic forms survived.

The 'Late Steam Age' witnessed the transition from steam to diesel traction and from semaphore to colour-light signalling. Electric multiple units (EMUs) ran alongside steam for some six decades and diesel multiple units (DMUs) for 15 years, while many colour-light systems dated from the 1920s and '30s. Elements of each can be found in some of the pictures. Steam locomotion is dominant, however, so too is mechanical signalling.

The book is divided into 70 mini-chapters of two facing pages, each taking a different theme (see Contents). Plate numbers are used throughout and are cross-referenced for the many 'composite' pictures which show several different sub-topics. Captions generally include the year, the nearest location (in bold type), and the pre-Grouping railway ownership. Only common abbreviations, such as for railway companies, have been used and are detailed in a glossary at the rear. The index of sub-topics is by plate number. The classifications of the Signalling Study Group (SSG) are used to identify signal box types (*Ref. 1*). All references used are listed at the rear, including the author's two volumes of *Odd Corners of the Southern* which many Southern modellers have already found useful (*Refs. 2* and *3*).

The author has been an enthusiast of real and model railways since 1943 (age three). One of his earliest memories is of a journey as an evacuee from Paddington to Cheltenham St James in a train packed with servicemen standing in the corridors. He acquired his first train set when aged four – a second-hand Hornby clockwork O gauge which included a four-wheel Pullman car named *Marjory*. He later progressed to Hornby Dublo, followed by kit-built OO gauge and then fine-scale EM gauge. His most ambitious layout was built during the 1980s in American N gauge (*Ref. 4*) which included a 12-wheel dining car called *La Croix*. His current project is a large tabletop layout using OO gauge Setrack, suitable for his grandchildren to assemble and enjoy (and making extensive use of this book for

Model Railway Detailing Manual

detailing). The trains include some delightful restaurant cars of the GWR, LMS and LNER (all made in China).

The author's interest in railway history and photography started when he left school to become an engineering apprentice. Living south of the Thames and with limited spare time and money, most of his exploration and research was of BR Southern Region and its predecessors. He nevertheless found the other railways of Britain and Europe equally interesting and took every opportunity to explore them. His most notable non-Southern outings were as follows:

• Field trips organised by Goldsmith's College to the Widened Lines (Met.) and to Temple Mills marshalling yard (GER).
• An RCTS railtour from Liverpool Street (GER) through London and North Kent.
• A week's holiday on the Norfolk Broads where steam trains and GER railway stations were photographed. (Sailing competed with railways at that time for the author's enthusiasm.)
• A week's holiday in the West Country, ostensibly to photograph Southern steam but inevitably encountering that 'other railway' – the Great Western.
• An exchange visit with engineering apprentices from Electricité de France provided an introduction to the SNCF at the Channel ports, in Paris, around Lyon and in the French Alps.
• A week's holiday on the Isle of Man, travelling to Liverpool on the Midland main line and then spent exclusively on the island's railways. Sadly, the sun rarely came out during that week.
• A three-week Grand Tour of the railways of the Netherlands, northern Germany, southern Belgium and northeast France. This was a 1960s equivalent of 'seeing the world'.
• A day out to Oxford, visiting the Thame branch (GWR) and returning via High Wycombe on the GWR/GCR joint line. Due to freezing fog, only a few of the photographs are clear.
• Six months living in Stafford while training with English Electric. Local photography included the LNWR, the NSR and a remote GNR branch (also the canals, but that is another story).
• Two trips to photograph railways on the Welsh borders while living in Stafford – the Cambrian, the Welshpool & Llanfair, the Shropshire & Montgomeryshire and the GWR/LNWR joint lines.
• Visits to the S&DJR and excursions to that lovely GWR branch line through Wells.
• Days out on the GER's Maldon branches and on the GWR line from Reading to Basingstoke.
• A few days based at Peterborough to savour steam on the GNR, MR, GER and LNWR.
• Visits to his fiancée's grandparents who lived in Stroud (GWR). Also with Marion, holidays in Tiverton (GWR), the Lake District (LNWR) and on honeymoon to Inverness (HR). Having no car, train rides and platform loitering were *absolutely necessary* during these holidays.

These outings were the source of many of the pictures in this book. In parallel with the above, the author walked or rode most of the

3 The SER works at **Ashford** opened for locomotives in 1847 and for carriages and wagons in 1850. The original entrance was beneath a brick clock tower with a bell tower added above. The lodge alongside was no doubt once occupied by a Superintendent. His two-storey villa in variegated brick is protected by a mesh fence and old sleepers. Photographed in 1959, the works closed in 1984. A similar tower and lodge once stood alongside Bristol Docks.

Introduction

Southern Region in search of steam. He only stopped intensive railway photography when BR steam came to an end and, simultaneously, he got married.

This ten-year odyssey of exploration and adventure is a testament of youth. While others enjoyed motorbikes and cars, or played sports or married early, the author chose railways as his passion of youth and savoured every moment. It was not until the early 1990s when he took early retirement that the railway negatives were unearthed and printed *en masse*, resulting in a series of pictorial books. A fundamental purpose of all his railway books has been to make his photographic collection generally available to others.

Love of the steam railway continues into the 21st century. Hundreds of thousands of people visit the preserved steam railways and museums each year, also the many miniature railways that you can ride on. Dozens of model railway exhibitions are enjoyed every month where steam outlines run on most of the layouts. This fascination with the steam age derives not simply from the fire, steam and motion of the drive but from all the beautiful detail that went with it – from panelled teak carriages and colourful private-owner wagons to ornate architecture, semaphore signals and friendly staff everywhere. The themes which follow illustrate some seven decades of railway development. I hope you enjoy this piece of social and industrial history. Please make good use of the detail to create model railways which are both authentic and captivating.

This is a pictorial book about real railways and for the practicalities of creating these artifacts in miniature, the reader should refer to the model railway manuals published by Haynes/PSL and others as well as the articles which appear each month in the many magazines.

Thanks are due to Marion for helping with the checking of the material.

Alan Postlethwaite
Stroud
January 2005

4 The rustic charm of **Wool** station on the LSWR main line to Weymouth. The two-storey brick building is enhanced by painted brick, dormer windows and a modest canopy with pointed valancing. The backward slope of the canopy is echoed in the shelter on the down side. Note the fire buckets, high-backed seats, posters and LSWR running-in board with its wooden cut-out letters. The up express is headed by SR light Pacific No. 34103 *Calstock*.

Station approaches

5 Not long after dawn in November 1958, a crewman comes off duty at **Ashford**, Kent. Two parcels vans, a small saloon and about 20 bicycles stand under the long canopy of the south forecourt. This was a surprisingly modest vernacular building for a major SER junction station. Today, this is the location of Ashford International.

6 No space for vehicles on the approach to **North Hayling** halt (LBSCR) on the Hayling Island branch. Passenger access is via a wicket gate and path. The larger gate serves a farm crossing. The lineside fencing was admirable in 1958.

7 The approach to **Brasted** (SER) was a long, metalled incline. In 1961, a gas lamp and a cast-iron sign guard the entrance. The modelling challenge here is realism of the trees and undergrowth.

8 On the NSR main line, the approach to **Stone** is in the vee of the junction. The right-hand fence is truncated to allow direct loading of goods – note the catch-point and BR ground-signal. A concrete footbridge, left, crosses the line from Stafford – the drying kilns beyond show that we are near the Potteries. The Jacobean style building is welcoming – see *Plate 9* for a close-up. In 1962, one Austin saloon and two bicycles stand on the forecourt. On the far right, a new shed has been built alongside the original brick goods shed.

Grand frontages

9 (*Right*): The NSR junction station of **Stone** has a compact, two-storey building of brick and stone in Jacobean style. The multiple round-topped mullioned windows are a delight, so too the entrance portico. The Flemish gables are finished with stone copings, finials and coats of arms. Chimneys are of modest height but with elaborate pots. The scene has a busy air with ladders up the wall, two stationmen at work and an open door to the parcels office.

10 (*Below*): The GER branch terminus of **Maldon East** was in Jacobean style. Most welcoming is the colonnade of nine arches in stone and brick, topped by a balcony with a balustrade and finials. The twin two-storey buildings are in bi-coloured brick, finished with Flemish gables and clusters of tall chimneys. Sadly in 1963, the branch was little-used, and soon to be axed. A stationman's car occupies an arch.

11 The MR's **Stamford Town** looks more like an ecclesiastical retreat than a railway building. Designed by Sancton Wood *(Ref. 5)*, the roof line and station house (right) are Tudor, but the windows and entrance arches of the single-storey offices are Gothic. The turret on the left is an aesthetic visual stop but is partly obscured by the lumber yard. In 1963, a BR van collects parcels.

12 Unusually for the LCDR, **Herne Hill** station has two storeys. The outline is Italianate but the Gothic window heads and courses of lighter brickwork are LCDR trademarks. In 1959, the SR name-sign was still in place; sections of clean brickwork suggest that the canopy was once longer. The saloon cars include an Austin Devon, a Standard and two Ford Consuls or Zephyrs.

Stone, brick and tiles

13 On the MR west of Stamford, **Ketton and Collyweston** has Tudor styling, but the middle room is a timber fill-in. The level-crossing room has a bay and a bell tower. Passing through in 1963, a mineral train is headed by LMS 8F class 2-8-0 No. 48696. The wooden signal post (left) is MR; the tubular steel post is LMS.

14 The LNWR line from Northampton was the first to reach Peterborough, opening in 1845. **Oundle** is in Tudor style, with elaborate tiling and clusters of chimneys. In 1963, a tender engine shunts in the yard by the staggered platform. Note the brick wall, oil lamps and wooden Way-out sign; both probably originals.

15 The ECR's **Peterborough East** opened in 1847, serving also the LNWR and MR. The buildings and company offices are in brick, Tudor style, with mullioned windows, corner stones and a three-arch entrance to the station. In 1963, two parcels vans, mail bags and barrows occupy the forecourt. The siding is unguarded.

16 Rebuilt in 1923 by Charles Clark, **Farringdon** has a neo-Classical outline covered in white glazed earthenware tiles known as faience. The 1920s name and company ownership are proudly incorporated. The Buffet sign behind the lamp-post leads to a first-floor restaurant. In 1962, there were four integral shops.

Multi-storey buildings

17 The buildings at **Ventnor West** on the Isle of Wight had faced stonework and round-headed windows in the Domestic Revival style, but were formerly obscured by a long platform canopy. The grand facilities, which included a buffet, seem excessive for this remote IWCR branch. Closed in 1953, a builder occupied this fine site in 1960.

18 Unusually for the SER, the Italianate building at **Sandwich** is two-storey in brick. By contrast, the shelter opposite is wooden vernacular. In Summer 1964, passengers shelter from the sun beneath the long SR canopy. Parcels are piled on the northbound platform and parcels vans occupy the siding.

19 The LNWR's two-storey building at **Nuneaton Trent Valley** was remarkably long and sombre. The plain Italianate outline in dark brick is relieved by the circular upper windows, an ornate clock tower, the Classical centre and a gable at the far end. A sense of grandeur is spoilt by the approach over a level crossing (to a goods yard) and by the oversized hoarding, advertising cigarettes, in 1962. A long plain canopy protects passengers and parcels.

20 On the SER's Hawkhurst branch, **Cranbrook** had an unusual three-storey brick house with dormer windows. It was set between the corrugated-steel booking office-waiting room and the low McK&H Type 3 signal box. In 1959, plants fill spaces around the porch, signal box and storage huts. The spiral-fluted lamp standards are SER.

Booking offices

21 *(Right)*: On the SR's Allhallows branch, this hut at **Stoke Junction Halt** was sometimes staffed. It incorporates both a shelter (left) and a booking office (right). The platform is prefabricated concrete but the hut is wooden on wooden piles. In 1960, no trains were advertised.

22 *(Below)*: In 1960 on the 3ft gauge IMR's Port Erin line, **Colby** had a larger and more attractive wooden building than Stoke Junction (above). The gable for the clock is a delight, mounted over the booking office. Beyond the porch is what looks like a waiting room. The setting includes a white fence, whitened stones for the flower beds, and trees to either side. There are no platforms – only a loading dock in the goods yard.

23 *(Opposite Top)*: On the LNWR line from Northampton to Peterborough, the brick booking office at **Barnwell** has a bay window for observing level-crossing traffic. The vernacular wooden waiting room with salient canopy looks much older. Arriving with a westbound train in 1963 is LNER B1 class 4-6-0 No. 61059.

24 *(Opposite Bottom)*: On the LSWR's North Devon line at **King's Nympton**, the booking office is sandwiched between the station house and the shelter. In 1959, all are adorned with wisteria and roses. The style is Tudor to the design of Sir William Tite. Note the LSWR barrow, bench seat, posters, SR signs and platform bell on the wall.

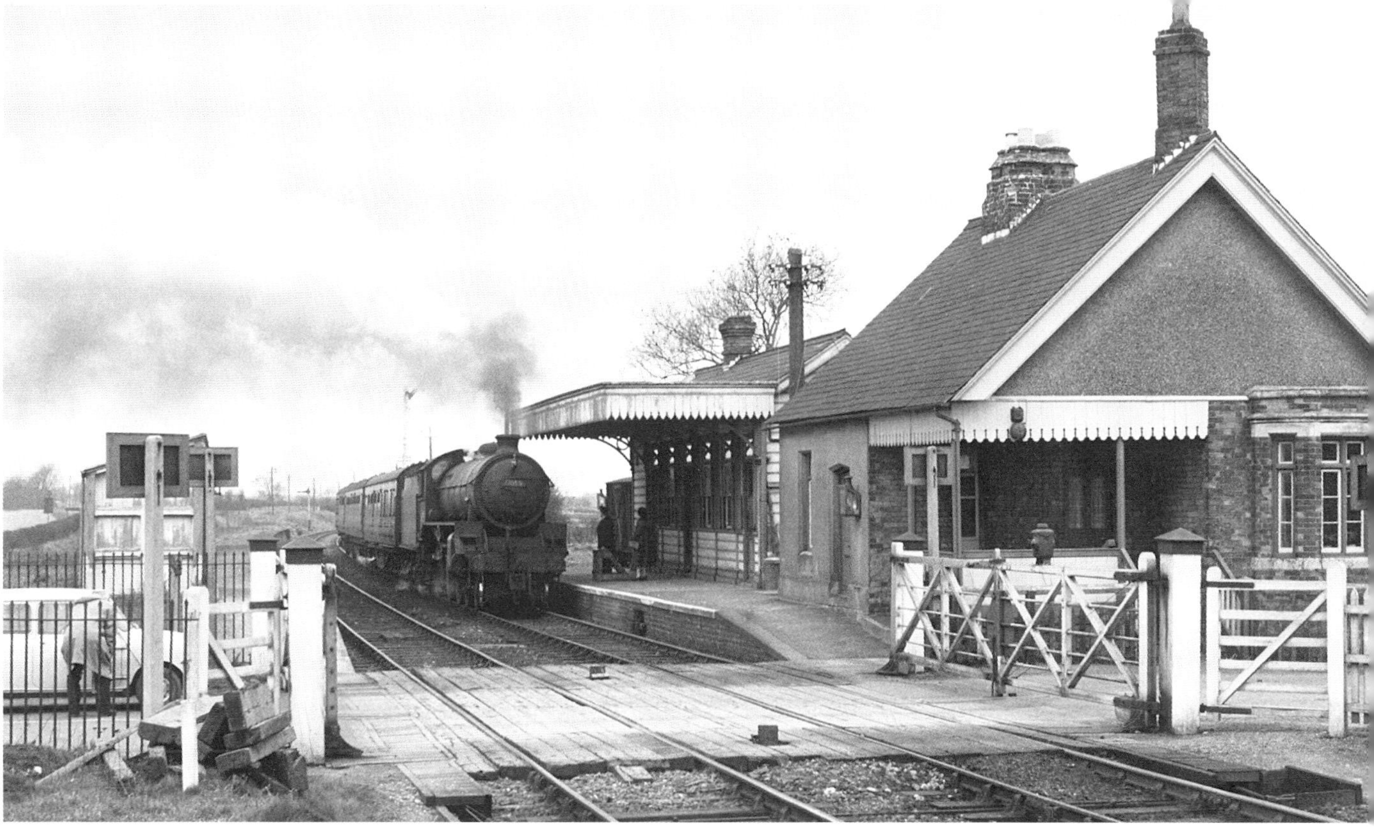

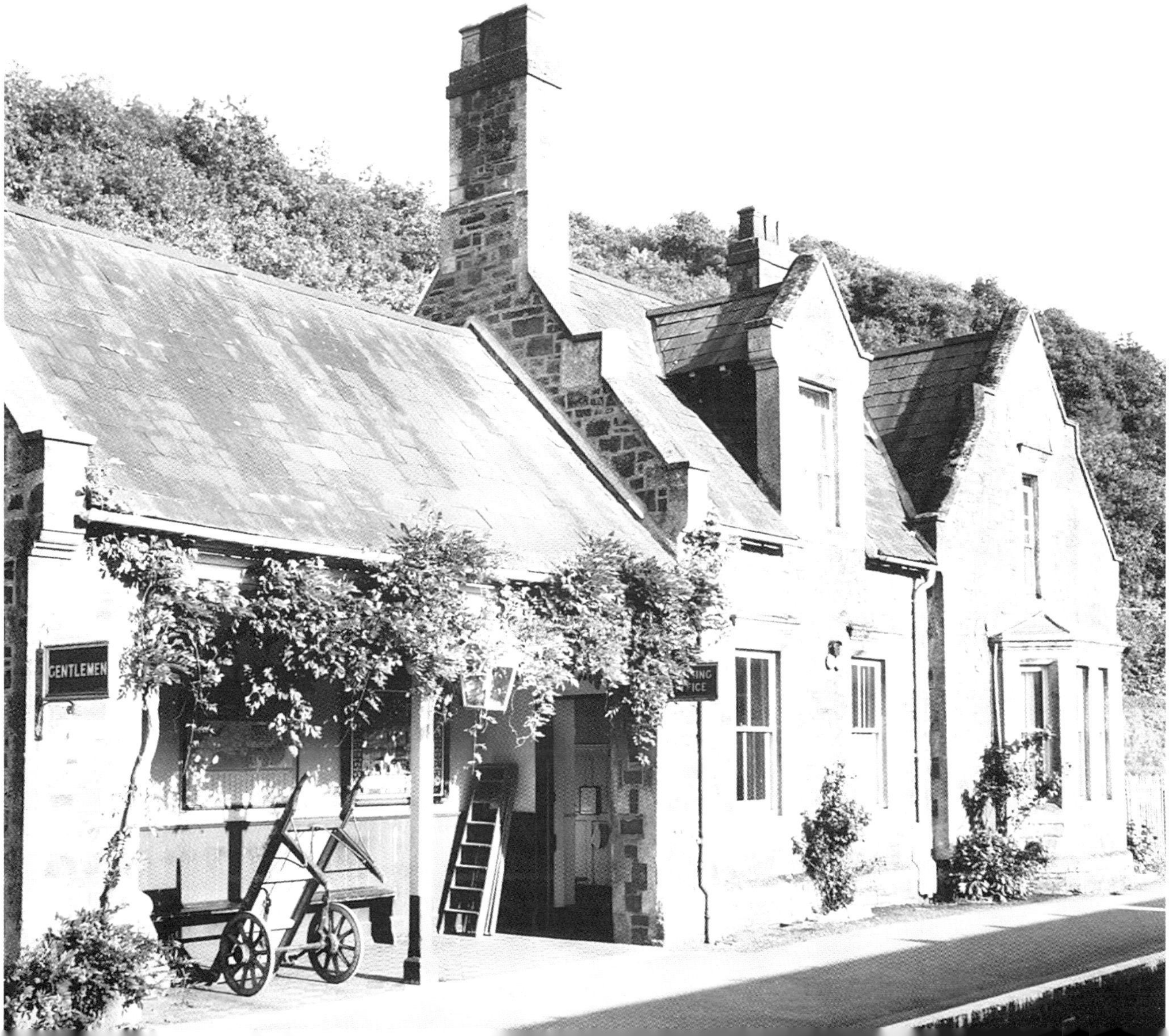
GENTLEMEN

Busy platforms

25 (*Above*): Passenger traffic on the Isle of Man is a mix of local people and seasonal visitors. On **Port St Mary**'s single platform, in the south of the island, a large gathering awaits the next train to Douglas. The station buildings are substantial, so too the goods shed with its fine stonework. Alas, goods traffic was minimal in 1960.

26 (*Below*): **Salisbury** was the first stop out of Waterloo for the 'Atlantic Coast Express', seen here in 1962 with rebuilt SR 'Merchant Navy' class heavy Pacific No. 35014 *Nederland Line*. Waiting for the stop are passengers, a porter, a water wagon (for toilet tanks) and the ice-cream lady. The platform is further embellished with barrows, concrete telegraph posts, loudspeakers and lamps. Empty stock stands alongside the large LSWR canopy, right.

27 (*Opposite, top*): The four platforms of **Waterloo (East)** were known as A, B, C and D. All eyes are upon the arrival of a six-car Hastings DEMU No. 1033, then considered the height of modernity. The third car incorporates a buffet. The substantial station canopies have SER valances and the electric lamps and standards are early SR (left) and late SR (right). As a backdrop, the Shell building is under construction, one of London's tallest buildings in 1960.

28 (*Below*): In 1959, rail enthusiasts circulate at **Canonbury** during an RCTS railtour (see *Plate 2*). EMUs for the North London line were built at Eastleigh (Southern Region) but with screw-link rather than buckeye outer couplings. A fragile railing protects passengers from the signal arms, mounted on a short NLR square wooden post. The footbridge is unusual, built *in situ* with a mix of iron, steel, bricks, concrete and wood.

Urban platforms

29 The two curved platforms at **Ryde Esplanade** has substantial canopies carried on rows of square posts. Owned jointly by the LBSCR and LSWR, the valancing is LSWR. The down valance (nearside) has been cropped, presumably to increase clearance when longer bogie stock was introduced. In 1960, LSWR O2 class 0-4-4T No. 32 *Bonchurch* heads a train of LSWR and LBSCR stock, all converted for Isle of Wight use.

30 Canonbury is a North London equivalent of Peckham Rye (opposite), having four platforms and a great Victorian mansion of a building. Being in a cutting, the platforms are solid and the island platform has the remnants of flower beds. The lamp (left) was fuelled by town gas in 1959. The flat NLR canopies are dilapidated and once adorned with valances. The electrified No. 2 lines (right) carried the regular passenger traffic.

31 A 4-SUB unit, No. 4286, from Sevenoaks to Holborn Viaduct arrives on the LCDR side of **Peckham Rye**. All four platforms, canopies and the great station building (right) which is located between two lines, were built by the LBSCR in a heavy Baroque style. For light weight, the elevated platforms were in timber. In 1960, the fences and shelters appear never to have been cleaned or repaired, but Wright's Coal Tar Soap shines through the begrimed enamel.

32 The GNR terminus at **Stamford** had a simple wooden peninsular platform for two lines with no locomotive release. The buffer-stop end was protected by a timber overall roof of steel trusses, partially glazed, carried on brick walls. The electric lighting looks woefully inadequate. The station has a goods yard (right), a carriage siding (to the left of the platelayers' hut) and an MPD beyond the signal box. All was deserted in 1963.

Salient canopies

33 In 1962, prior to the installation of OHE and colour-light signalling, the canopies at **Nuneaton Trent Valley** were rebuilt. Temporary wooden supports are in place on the island platform, but the original LNWR cast-iron columns would be retained. Shunting on the right is an LMS 'Jinty' 0-6-0T. Beyond the great bridge, the station is guarded by a forest of LNWR and LMS signals on tall brackets and posts.

34 The canopy at **Shepton Mallet High Street** is salient in that it juts out noticeably. In common with many GWR stations, however, its cantilevered support beams are integral with the station roof, requiring only small holding brackets. In 1962, GWR signals, signs and a barrow adorn the platforms. Although the line becomes single beyond the bridge, the siding adheres to the principle of 'no facing points on running lines'.

35 This pitched-roof canopy at **Uttoxeter** (NSR) could be mistaken for an open barn. Timber-built and wide, it is supported by the booking office wall and by a row of cast-iron columns. In 1962, passengers are scarce as LMS 2-6-4 tank No. 42609 prepares to depart with a train to Leek via the Churnet Valley.

36 The down canopy at **Sheffield Park** was an afterthought of timber, supported on square wooden posts. It semi-obscures the Old English style of the station building – partly hung with courses of plain and fish-scale tiles. The ornate chimney stacks and the fine carving on the gable end of the extension are a credit to the LBSCR. Photographed in 1959 when the Bluebell Railway preservation project was in its infancy.

Integral canopies

37 From the MR's **Nuneaton Abbey Street**, lines ran northwards to Burton, Derby, Coalville, Loughborough (LNWR) and Leicester (via the LNWR). In 1962, a DMU approaches from Leicester on a Birmingham service. The main building has a neat, restful style – a single-storey Italianate villa with a shallow-angled hipped roof, plain rectangular chimneys, elegant modillions under the eaves and tall ornate windows with arced heads. The central shelter with intermediate supports a canopy which is integral with the main roof. Smaller rooms at the sides provide balance, including the Gents at the far end. See *Plate 53* for a night picture here.

38 The LCDR's **Bat and Ball** has a welcoming frontage. Its integral architecture incorporates the station house (far end), the booking office (near end); and a linking waiting room whose extended roof makes an entrance canopy. Final touches are provided by the elaborate multicoloured brickwork and Gothic windows with pointed heads (see also *Plate 12*). In 1961, the only hint of activity is a motorised bicycle.

39 This GWR cantilevered canopy at **Littlemore** reaches to the platform edge. Viewed from the side, it is an integral part of the roof structure whereas Nuneaton's canopy (opposite) is integral when viewed from the front. In 1962, a mixed goods train passes through. The lamp with its pulleys appears broken, but the wooden nameboard is fine, so too is the flower bed. See *Plates 57* and *93* for further pictures on this line.

40 This booking office-waiting room at **Shapwick** looks like a Central Somerset Railway original (a constituent of the S&DJR). Although vernacular in timber and slate, it has architectural merit by virtue of the small integral canopy (an extension of the main roof). Photographed in 1963, the concrete platform is SR.

Open footbridges

Most footbridges were supplied by contractors. They were generally prefabricated and transported in sections for assembly on site. Wooden footboards and lamps were then added and renewed periodically.

41 *(Right)*: **Launceston** had an unusual combination of stone side-steps to a lattice steel arch made in two sections. On a morning train to Padstow in 1959, LSWR T9 class 4-4-0 No. 30717 awaits the green flag. Note the water column, brazier and SR concrete fence.

42 *(Below)*: On the HR at **Nairn**, this lattice footbridge would have

been transported to site in five main sections: the span, two towers with tubular columns; and two flights of side-steps. The lamp standards would once have held oil lamps. The footbridge is beautifully painted and looks in mint condition. (The life of steel and iron is indefinite if painted regularly.) In 1967, a Swindon-built DMU arrives from Forres. A mail van and milk churns await loading (possibly the train will draw forward to the guard's compartment, see *Plate 90*). Note the two types of barrow under the footbridge, left. Cowes on the Isle of Wight had a footbridge of this design, suggesting a common supplier (*Plate 68*).

43 Prefabricated platforms, footbridges and other structures were made at the SR's concrete works at Exmouth Junction. The bridges were ultramodern but few were needed since the steel ones were so durable. At **Chilham** (north of Ashford, Kent), such a bridge enhances the scene, together with Sugg Rochester gas lamps (with home-made steps). The SER building and shelter are modest. In 1964, the loading dock appears to be disused but the goods yard beyond is active. Note the banner repeater signals and the toppled speed restriction signs, right.

44 Riveted steel plate is sometimes used for the sides, especially where the footbridge is a public right-of-way rather than a passenger crossing, as at the London end of **Southampton Central**. The tall sides on the bridge protect pedestrians from locomotive exhaust and reduce the risk of missiles aimed at passing trains. In cross-section, the bridge is a U-shape beam supported on brick plinths. For a neat finish, the right-hand plinth is rendered in plasticised mortar, as are the sides of the steps. In 1963, two stop signals on rail-built posts frame Ivatt Class 2MT 2-6-2T No. 41276. Although the bridge sides are tall, the author could just reach up for a photograph (see *Plate 154* for the view eastwards).

Covered footbridges

45 A box-girder bridge design uses the roof as a structural component. Spanning four tracks, this 1938 bridge at **Havant** would have come in two parts. Offices are built into the towers. Some footbridges of this type also had a goods lift opposite each staircase. In 1959, 2-BIL unit No. 2067 from Brighton graces the long platform.

46 This lattice bridge at **Sydenham Hill** has low side-boards and a lightweight corrugated roof, giving partial weather protection. New SR platform canopies have been built on the original LCDR columns. In 1959, the author's sister waits patiently as passengers board 4-SUB unit No. 4122 to Victoria. 'Is it time to go, yet?'

47 This fully enclosed footbridge at **Sittingbourne** has a lightweight pitched roof (not box-girder). The tall windows are non-opening and a catwalk is provided for external cleaning. In 1959, SR N class Mogul No. 31402 heads a train of BR Mark 1 stock, bound for Thanet. Note the awkward, 90° turn in the roofing.

48 This early Brunel station at **Stroud** is now Grade 2 listed. The GWR footbridge has plated sides with frosted glass extensions, together with a lightweight corrugated roof and a deep valance, leaving just a small ventilation gap. In 1964, a GWR motor-train from Chalford to Gloucester is propelled by 0-4-2 tank No. 1453.

Platform shelters

49 *(Opposite, top)*: All three stations (opposite) closed under Beeching. Near Stroud, **Downfield Crossing Halt** served four schools. It had two GWR pagoda-type shelters made of corrugated galvanised steel. In 1964, a GWR motor-train approaches, headed by an 0-4-2 tank.

50 *(Opposite, middle)*: On the S&DJR at **Stalbridge**, the simple shelter had a backward-sloping roof and canopy. Note the flower beds. In 1963, BR Standard Class 5MT 4-6-0 No. 73054 heads a four-coach set.

51 *(Opposite, bottom)*: Opened by the SECR in 1905 on the SER's Westerham branch, **Chevening Halt** was rebuilt by the SR in prefabricated concrete. Unusually, the shelter has a pitched roof.

52 *(Above, right)*: Some fine buildings could be found on the IWCR's Ventnor West line. At **Whitwell**, seven years after closure, this cottage-style shelter still enhanced the down platform in 1960. Although ivy, grass and climbing shrubs are encroaching, the pebbledash walls and overhung pitched roof remain distinctive.

53 *(Below)*: In 1962, this shelter at **Nuneaton Abbey Street** was called a waiting room, but lacked a door. Clues to MR ownership are the 45° slats of the fence and the fine brickwork – built to last a thousand years. Note the paving across the gravel platform leading to the shelter. The lamp standard on the left would once have carried an oil lamp. (See also *Plate 37*.)

Platform lamps

54 *(Right)*: By the cattle pens at **Thame**, this GWR lamp standard is fluted at the bottom and plain circular above. In 1962, the cradle carried an oil lantern converted to town gas (with a new pipe at the bottom). The lantern design is near-identical to those on the SER at Cliffe (*Ref. 2*), having a front name panel, ornate top corners and a finial on the cowl (air vent) at the top.

55 *(Below)*: **Oxted** was always an elegant, civilised station with its tall chimneys and SER arc-roof canopies. It also boasted a fine set of early SR spiral-fluted lamp standards. Fitted with Sugg Rochester gas lamps, they were pole-operated (the pilot flame was always alight). In 1962, the waiting passenger on the right carries the standard commuting kit of briefcase, umbrella, *Daily Telegraph*, bowler hat and gaberdine raincoat of the era. His push-pull connection to the Hever line is fast approaching on the crossover from the up road.

56 When **Hastings** was modernised in 1931, the two island platforms were adorned with electric lamps and concrete standards in art deco style. The signals and signal box are also SR – the side and the closet of the latter are glinting in the evening sunshine. The great lattice road bridge leads up to a fine mansion (ideal for engine-spotting in the days of steam). In 1961, a humble SR 2-BIL unit approaches from Ore to Brighton.

57 This GWR lamp standard at **Thame** carries a Sugg Rochester gas light in a cradle. The operating wires have been extended to avoid the need for a pole. The water column beyond has a top truss (see *Plates 303-306* for further water columns). An atmospheric view in freezing fog in January 1962 shows GWR Prairie tank No. 6123 heading a local train.

Botanic platforms

58 *(Right)*: Many S&DJR platforms were adorned with small flower beds, retained by stones. At **Evercreech Junction** in 1963, they enhance the departure of an up train headed by a BR Standard Class 5MT 4-6-0 and a BR full brake. The gradient of the line can be judged against the level siding beyond.

59 *(Below)*: **Craven Arms and Stokesay** was enhanced by flower beds, tubs and ornamental grasses. In 1962, a train from Shrewsbury is headed by a 'Warship' class B-B diesel-hydraulic. The canopy brackets are as fine as lace at this joint GWR/LNWR station. The lamp standards and name-signs are BR, the seat is GWR

60 On the Trent Valley line at **Barlaston & Tittensor**, platform flower beds are retained by dry stone walls. In March 1962, wallflowers on the right are not yet in bloom. The scene is further enhanced by NSR seats, white fencing and a barrow. All are dominated by the bold Tudor architecture of the station building.

61 Backed by hedging and trees, lupins glorify this GER staggered platform at **Brundall**. In 1959, a Norwich to Yarmouth local train pauses for imaginary passengers. The tall front windows of the Derby-built 'lightweights' made them strong contenders for the most attractive design of BR's first-generation DMUs.

Station signs

62 *(Right)*: A two-piece BR running-in board at **Dunton Green** in 1960. The SER Westerham branch closed in 1961.

63 *(Below, left)*: In 1964, a booking office sign at **Whitstable & Tankerton** (LCDR) - for sprightly passengers!

64 *(Below, right)*: A poster at **Port Soderick**, Isle of Man, photographed in 1960 but advertising the pre-1948 LMS overnight ferry service to Dunkerque via Liverpool, St Pancras and Harwich.

65 *(Above)*: In 1962, a seven-piece BR enamelled nameboard at **Craven Arms and Stokesay**. The Central Wales line escaped the Beeching axe and is highly scenic.

66 *(Left)*: In 1961, BR enamelled Danger signs in three languages at **Dover Marine**.

67 *(Below)*: LMS nameboards at Rocester (NSR) in 1962. The wooden post with the electric lamp would once have carried an oil lantern.

Branch termini

68 The main platform at **Cowes** is on the left. A dwarf semaphore signal guards the locomotive release crossover. The sharp curvature requires check-rails on both lines. The footbridge is a public right of way, not for passengers. In 1960, the platforms are empty except for two barrows. An SECR coach stands beyond the SR concrete nameboard – still painted with wartime white bands. This IWCR terminus closed in 1966. Its compactness makes it ideal for modelling. Note the terraced cottages which are bisected by the station.

69 Addiscombe had a single peninsular platform with SR gas lamps and standards. After electrification in 1926, the run-round loop (left) became a carriage siding; EPB units are seen here in 1958. Opened by the SER in 1864, it closed in the mid-1990s when the Croydon Tramlink took over most of the branch.

70 The run-round point at **Ramsey** is alongside this simple stone-built engine shed and water tower. In 1960, 2-4-0 tank No. 13 *Kissack* runs round the train from Douglas. This port was once busy with freight traffic, carrying Cumberland coal to Foxdale (*Plate 80*) and lead ore on the return journey. The MNR line to Ramsey closed in 1968.

71 Llanfyllin had a classic single-platform configuration with a locomotive run-round and a goods yard. The station building was exceptionally large for such a remote terminus, suggesting CR optimism for traffic growth. Traffic was light when visited in 1962; the branch closed under Beeching.

Country stations

72 (*Right*): On the CR's Llanfyllin branch, **Llanfechain** had a two-storey brick house with a small canopy. A wooden name-sign stands in front of the booking office. The short platform has a dock extension with an animal pen. On Whitsun weekend in 1962, the scene is enhanced by a bank of cow parsley, a tall tree and grass in the dock. Such a setting is well suited for modelling, suggesting a fiddle yard beyond the stone bridge.

73 (*Below*): The LBSCR built some substantial, attractive country stations. This two-storey stationman's house at **Hever** has courses and eaves of coloured brick, round-headed windows and fancy chimneys. The triangular canopies and valances are also neat. The concrete platelayers' huts are of SR design. In 1963, SECR H class 0-4-4 tank No. 31518 restarts with a Maunsell push-pull set from Tunbridge Wells West to Oxted.

74 On the GWR secondary line south of Reading, **Bramley** station is dominated by the great canopy which is cantilevered from the single-storey building. The subtle curvature of the valance is echoed in the much smaller canopy on the platform opposite. In 1963, all is neat and tidy but deserted. Note the new BR running-in board, and the lamp standards in SR art-deco style. This line had been absorbed into the Southern Region.

75 On the LNWR secondary line from Stafford to Wellington, the long platforms at **Gnosall** have been extended twice – having two solid sections at different levels plus one wooden section. Mid-platform are flower beds, although not yet in bloom, in April 1962. Each wooden building has an integral canopy beneath a tall arc roof – a cheap but unappealing design. By contrast, the LNWR wooden nameboard has character.

Complete halts

76 On the GER's Maldon branch, a Metro-Cammell two-car DMU departs **Langford & Ulton** for Witham. The halt comprises a simple wooden canopy, a bench, a short solid platform with iron railings, two oil lamps on iron standards and a wooden nameboard. In 1963, grass was starting to grow on the platform.

77 Bryngwyn was on the CR's Llanfyllin branch. Provisions are similar to Langford (above) except that the shelter is enclosed in corrugated metal to give better weather protection, and the platform is in prefabricated concrete. In 1962, the oil lamps are, left to right, tapered, missing and rectangular.

78 Whereas Bryngwyn (opposite) was the last halt on the Llanfyllin branch, **Carreghofa** was the first, just outside Llanynymech. It was a late addition, built by the GWR and seen here in 1962 in excellent condition. The railings, lamp standard and nameboard are of the same pattern as at Bryngwyn but the shelter and railing posts are wooden and the platform is solid – topped with gravel and edged with timbers.

79 An unadvertised works halt on the NSR's Trent Valley line was **Wedgwood Halt**, serving the renowned ceramics factory. The long wooden platforms are supported on concrete blocks. The fences, gates and shelters are also wooden. In 1962, the lamps were an odd mix of electric (up line, left) and oil (down line, right).

Station trackwork

80 (*Right*): A simple run-round loop at **Foxdale**. The Foxdale Railway was leased to the MNR. It served five lead mines and a slate quarry. Mineral trains ran to Ramsey port, returning with Cumberland coal for the mine pumps. This was the first line to close on the Isle Man and by 1960, the station house was a private residence. A Land Rover is parked on the platform and the trackwork is grass-infested.

81 (*Below*): **Allhallows-on-Sea** was a bleak Thames-side resort with caravans and a few buildings. The peninsular platform had run-round loops. There was a small goods yard and a turntable to the right of the scissors crossover. Once double-track as far as Stoke Junction, it had regressed to single-line working by 1960.

82 (*Above*): On the SER's Westerham branch, 23½ miles from Charing Cross, **Brasted** had three sidings. The facing point and catch-point are operated from a ground-frame via the rods and cranks on the right. For the point to operate, the plunger must first be withdrawn. This is operated by the rods and cranks on the left via a lifting lockbar fitted alongside the left-hand rail. This bar will only lift when no wheels are upon it, thereby ensuring safe operation of the point.

83 (*Above, right*): A mile from the village that it served, **Cliffe** was a passing station on the SR's Allhallows branch. SER boat trains once raced through here to Port Victoria on the Medway. The station house, booking office and up canopy are substantial. Instead of a footbridge, there is a passenger foot crossing at the far end.

84 (*Below*): A possible prototype for a space-restricted model railway, this unique track arrangement at **Wells** had a GWR branch line crossing the sidings of the S&DJR goods yard. The closed S&DJR platform can be seen on the right. Beyond the level-crossing was the East Somerset terminus which closed in 1878. To the left was the Bristol & Exeter's Tucker Street, the only passenger station to survive in 1962. The GWR built this curious connection when it took over the East Somerset and the B&E, converting to standard gauge at the same time.

Closed stations

85 (*Above*): The S&MR closed to passengers in 1933 and to all traffic in 1960. In 1962, the S&M platform roads at **Llanymynech** were in use as goods sidings (right). The double-track Cambrian main line sweeps through beneath a footbridge of generous stair-width. Note the one-wheel barrow and the two styles of shelter.

86 (*Below*): The joint GWR/LNWR **Minsterley** branch closed to passengers in 1951. At the terminus in 1962, wagons stand to either side of a new goods shed while a black cat guards the old station building.

87 (*Opposite, top*): The S&MR crossed the River Severn near **Ford & Crossgates**. In 1962, the wooden building and a wagon body rot away on the bi-level platform. The white board looks like a signal siting shield.

88 (*Opposite, middle*): The short NSR excursion branch line to Trentham Gardens closed in 1957. Nicely faced in brick, the branch platform at **Trentham** had its own waiting room. They stand apart from the NSR main line platforms and goods yard (left). In 1962, assorted hopper wagons occupied the truncated branch.

89 (*Opposite, bottom*): On the joint GWR/LNWR line south of Shrewsbury, **Dorrington** closed to passengers in 1958. Four years later, the platforms are chamfered off but the yard remains active with milk traffic and general goods. The old station buildings are in a restful Italianate style with unusual windows.

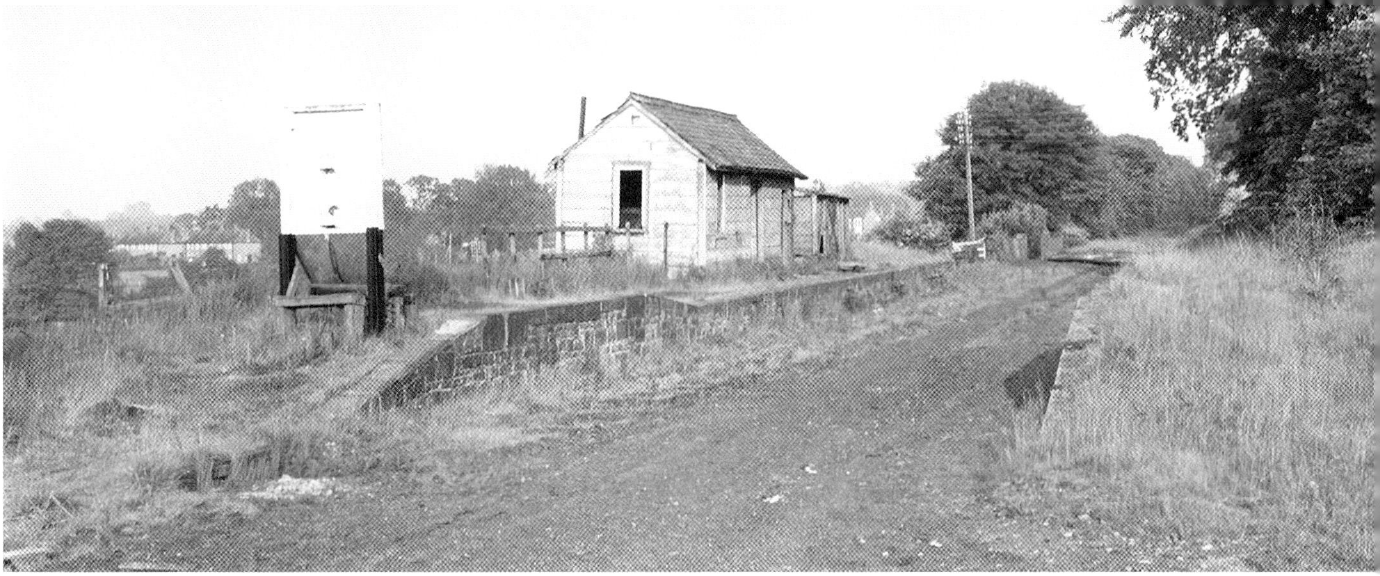

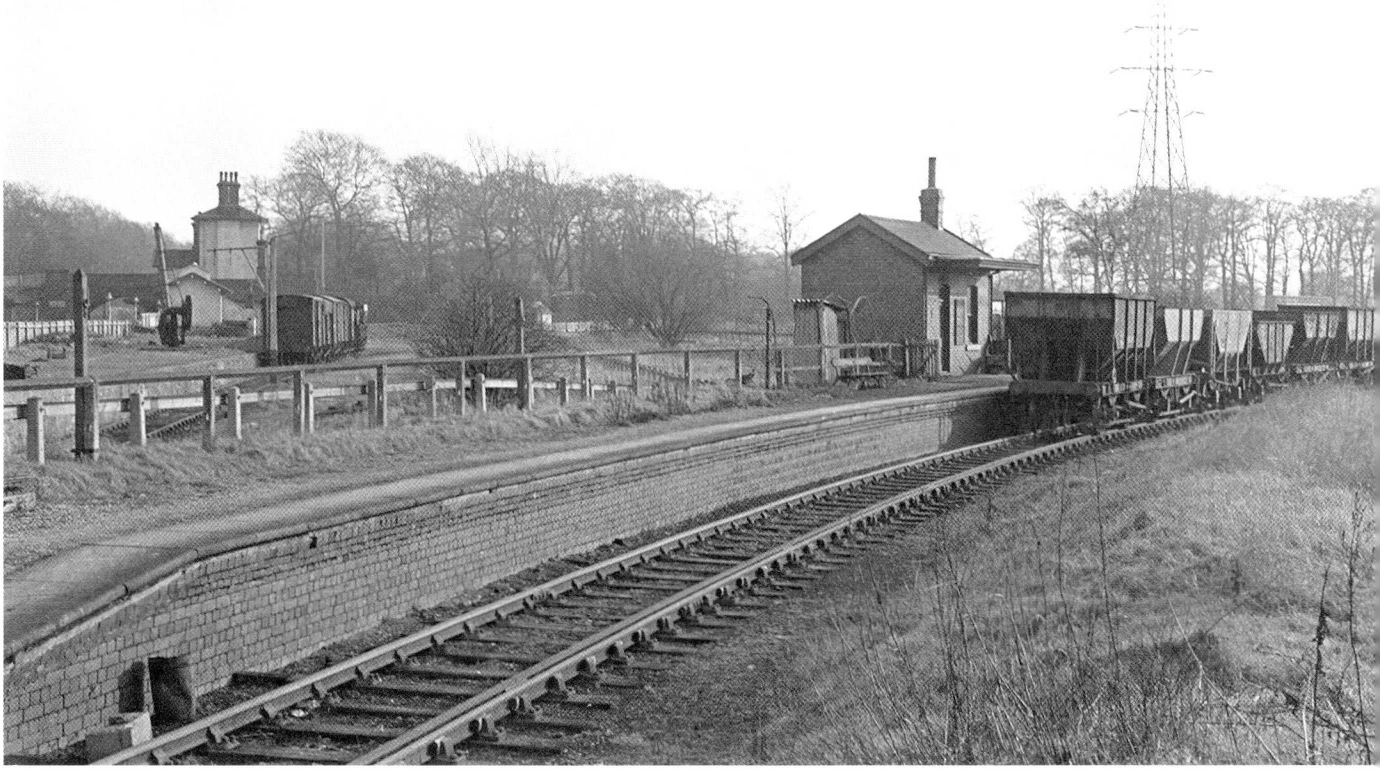

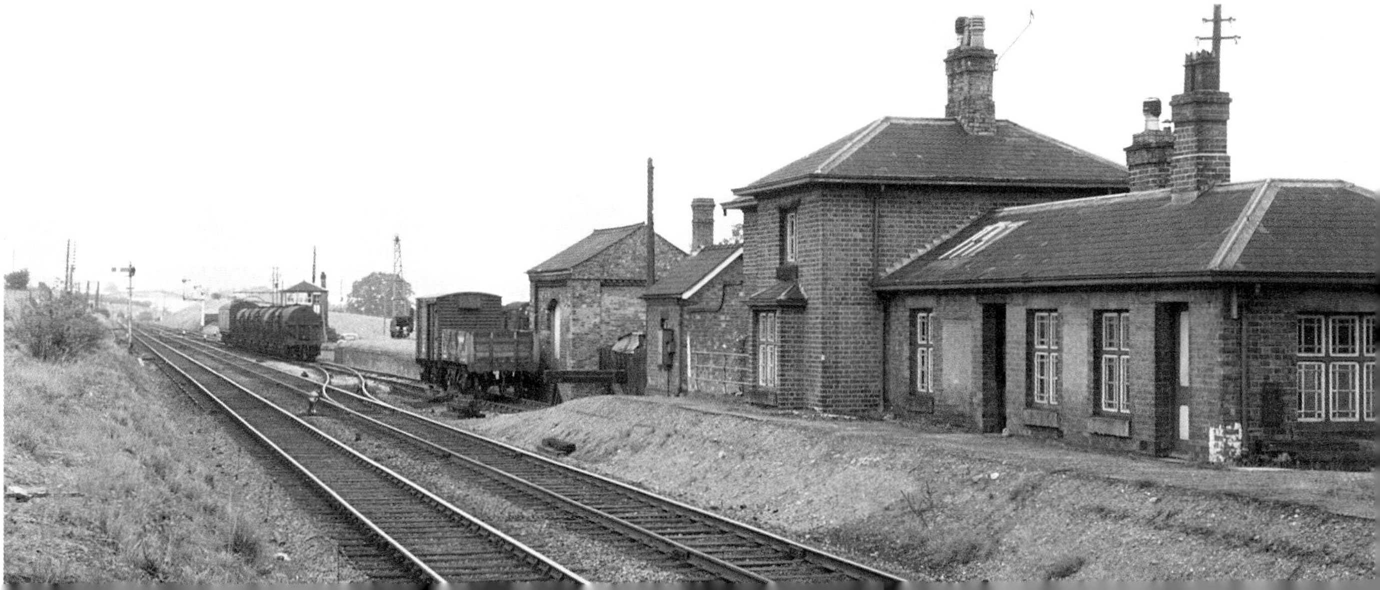

Platform barrows

90 (*Right*): In 1962, at the MR's **Nuneaton Abbey Street**, a DMU to Birmingham has drawn forward so that milk churns can be loaded readily into the guard's compartment from a waiting four-wheel barrow. One wonders where were the farm and creamery? The train comprises two three-car Cravens units. See *Plates 37* and *53* for further pictures of the station building and waiting room.

91 (*Below*): **Portsmouth & Southsea** low-level platforms 1 and 2 are stacked with parcels and Waterloo coach-boards. The barrows are: a GWR four-wheeler (left); an LSWR two-wheeler (centre); and several SR four-wheelers (right). The SR glazed canopy is supported on brackets from central girders. In 1961, the contrasting DMUs are a diesel-mechanical from the Western Region (left) and diesel-electric No. 1124 from the Southern Region.

92 Two-wheel barrows and a seat on the NSR at **Mow Cop & Scholar Green** (north of Stoke). In 1962, the staggered platform is further embellished with white fencing, a small tree, a flower bed and the backward-sloping propped canopy. The tubular steel signal post is LMS and the signal box is an NSR Type 2.

93 On a raw January day in 1962, GWR 2-6-2 tank No. 6123 draws into **Littlemore** (just south of Oxford). Snow is piled on the platform and the edge is gritted. GWR patterns are evident in the wooden signs, canopy valance and three types of barrow – single-wheel, two-wheel and four-wheel (behind the wall).

Parcels and mails

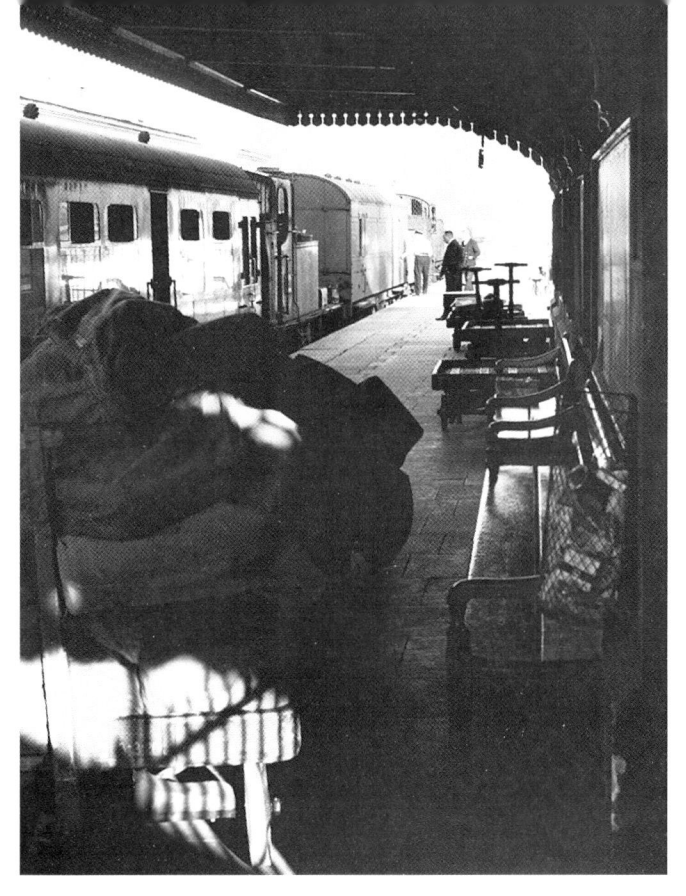

94 (*Above, left*): Near **Penkridge** (LNWR), in 1962, a short parcels train is headed by LMS Class 5MT 'Black Five' 4-6-0 No. 45114. The consist is a BR bogie parcels van and a private bogie wagon of Palethorpes Pork Sausages.

95 (*Above, right*): Mail bags are piled on the down platform at **Stroud** in 1964. A BR four-wheel parcels van has been shunted from an up bay on to the rear of the motor-train, en route to Gloucester. The locomotives are GWR Prairie tank No. 6128 and Collett 0-4-2T No. 1453. Note the GWR seats and four-wheel barrows.

96 (*Below*): In 1963, a mail train from Waterloo arrives at **Weymouth** headed by rebuilt 'Merchant Navy' Pacific No. 35011 *General Steam Navigation*. It comprises five Bulleid passenger coaches and four parcels vans – three BR and one GWR. Note the disc type ground signals and point lever for the central sidings.

97 At **Colwich Junction** in 1962, a 'fitted' parcels train speeds towards Stafford with a mix of coaches, parcels vans and goods vans. New OHE catenary has been erected but is not yet in commission. The NSR's Trent Valley line branches off to the right. The closed station was joint LNWR/NSR; its stone building is in Jacobean style, having gables similar to those on the NSR at Stone (*Plate 9*).

98 On the SER near **Poll Hill Tunnel** in 1960, a down parcels train is headed by SR 'Schools' class 4-4-0 No. 30927 *Clifton*. It comprises a four-wheel parcels van and a pair of straight-sided corridor coaches, all built under Richard Maunsell. The 45° cutting has spring flowers, a few shrubs and two rows of telegraph poles.

Goods shed layouts

99 On the HR at **Nairn**, the goods yard had direct entry from the down line. The shed is on a short spur. In 1967, a diesel locomotive leaves the rear of its train on the up line in order to shunt in the yard. The platforms are semi-staggered with a trailing crossover alongside the fine single-storey station building. Note the integral canopy, the shuttered bookstall, the bay window of the waiting room, and the circular flower beds. The stationman's house stands beyond with its dormer windows. The line becomes single beyond the signal box.

100 The GWR yard at **Stroud** had direct entry from the up line but via a double-slip point instead of the simple points seen at Nairn (above). The Cotswold stone shed is on a loop with the goods office at one end and the signal box at the other (an S&F Type 1). In 1964, a 'Western' class diesel-hydraulic locomotive runs light past the down home signal and a coal siding. A funeral cortège of condemned steam locomotives is held in the main yard (see *Plate 313*). Thankfully, the goods shed and its office are now Grade 2 listed, but the signal box has gone.

101 Four Crosses was on the CR main line south of Llanymynech. It had a neat arrangement of staggered platforms with a passenger foot crossing. The simple brick station buildings have direct barrow access from the paved platform into the goods shed. Shiny rails indicate regular use of the goods yard. Two crossovers connect to the goods siding, an arrangement made simple by the singling of the line in the distance. In 1962, a lone railwayman sees off a southbound train. The signal box is a Dutton Type 1, but with GWR windows.

102 The SR and its constituents generally avoided direct entry from running lines into local goods yards. On the LCDR main line at **Shepherds Well**, entry is by trailing points to a long holding siding (left) and to the down yard (right). Goods were handled in the brick shed and in a cattle dock where a diesel shunter stands with a brake van, in 1961. The marshalling sidings were for coal trains from the EKR line to Tilmanstone Colliery. The station buildings are simple but neat with an integral canopy.

Goods stations

103 (*Right*): The GNR's **Farringdon Goods** station was alongside the Met. passenger station (left). It connected to the Widened Lines via a goods yard (behind the camera). The shed roof was originally glazed. The cobbled yard gave direct access to the warehouse on the right. Wagons were once drawn via ropes and bollards – one can be seen on the right with another keeled over on the left. The enamelled sign reads 'Engines must condense'. All was in a sad state of decay in 1959, ripe for redevelopment.

104 (Below): **Ashford West** became goods-only after the SECR merger of 1899. The old LCDR passenger platforms on the right once had canopies. The long brick shed was used originally for carriage storage, having a central platform. In late 1958, stabled wagons included cattle, steel open, wooden open, double bolster and brake vans.

105 In 1963, the MR goods station at **Stamford Town** was busy with both local and through traffic. Between the goods shed and the signal box (right), assorted wagons and brake vans stand in the yard while LMS Class 4F 0-6-0 No. 44130 prepares to depart with a mixed goods train towards Peterborough.

106 The first railway station to serve Portsmouth was at **Gosport**, but had to be reached by ferry. Its prestigious passenger building was in neo-Classical style. A triangular truss roof covered the ends of two platforms – goods on the left and passengers on the right. Opened by the LSWR in 1841, it was singled in 1934 and became goods-only in 1953. This 1958 scene looks busy, with over twenty wagons visible on eight sidings. The signal box is a late LSWR Type 4 with its locking room windows bricked up. Signals on the branch had been dismantled but wooden staging remained over the point rods, formerly used for the single-track tablet exchange.

Loading the goods

107 Sandwich (SER) had a large goods shed with a canopy on either side. Outside the shed are a swinging jib crane and a (non-travelling) overhead crane for container wagons. In 1963, grass encroaches on the sidings and the rail-built buffer-stops. Beyond, the station footbridge stands out in a flat landscape.

108 This ornate GWR loading gauge at **Whitchurch Town** has chain-operated hinged side pieces. The post is a pair of bullhead rails. In 1963, a diesel-hauled up heavy goods train approaches, framed by the loading gauge, water column and stop signal. The signal box is a GWR Type 13; built of brick with a concrete roof, it is plain and simple to ARP specifications (Air Raid Precautions during the Second World War).

109 This LMS loading gauge at **Stamford Town** has steel components bolted to a ferro-concrete post. On a murky morning in 1963 it frames a mixed freight train headed by LMS Class 4F 0-6-0 No. 44130. The long road bridge comprises a simple steel beam with plated sides and railings, supported on brick pillars.

110 This large goods shed at **Nine Elms** was purpose-built by the LSWR. Its roof is a masterpiece of steel trusses with generous glazing. Electric lighting comprises two meagre rows of tungsten lamps covering the two platforms, but not the central cobbled road. The latter was designed for carts and drays rather than for much longer motor-lorries. Mechanical horse trailers are a good fit, however, four or five of which are seen here. The two rows of jib cranes are chain operated – goods handling was entirely manual here in 1961. The nearest trailer advertises day excursions to the South Coast – excellent value for railway photographers at 12/- to 14/- (60p to 70p). For maximum value on such journeys, the author would often rise before dawn and return home after dark.

Marshalling yards

111 Sharnal Street sidings were used to marshal trains to and from the Kingsnorth Light Railway (behind the camera) and the Chattenden Naval Tramway – straight ahead, under the bridge. The former carried mainly chemicals and closed in 1940. The latter was used by munitions trains for ships at Chatham Dockyard, and closed in 1961. Just one wagon was evident in 1958, with grass taking over the sidings. The SR's Allhallows-on-Sea branch is on the right, with Sharnal Street's up home signal raised. A gate once led from the yard.

112 Near Lea Bridge in north east London, **Temple Mills** hump yard was built by BR on the site of former GER marshalling yards. Wagons are sorted and retarded remotely from a central control tower. Here, a BR goods van (fitted for continuous braking) runs by gravity over a secondary retarder to a balloon of six sorting sidings. A bank of pneumatic cylinders operates a clamp on each rail. The central operator selects the braking pressure according to the speed and weight of each wagon and the distance that it must travel to buffering. Although suitable for computer control, this had not been developed when visited in 1958.

113 The sidings at the Cowes end of **Newport** were used for carriage storage, general Isle of Wight marshalling and the pre-sorting of wagons for the space-restricted Medina Wharf. In April 1960, five- and seven-plank wooden open wagons are dominant. Sleepers, old and new, are stacked liberally in the foreground.

114 Three low-sided steel wagons roll down the hump at **Temple Mills** marshalling yard. They will pass over one of two primary retarders this side of the control tower, then over one of eight secondary retarders into 47 sidings. Goods engines descend to the left and the diesel shunter return is on the right

Shifting coal

115 (*Bottom*): On the NSR main line near **Trentham** in 1962, LMS Class 5MT 4-6-0 No. 44871 heads a coal train from the North Staffordshire coalfield to a power station further south, possibly Meaford (see *Plate 153*).

116 (*Opposite, top*): Near **Wedgwood Halt** in 1962, LMS 'Crab' 2-6-0 No. 42887 runs tender-first with a train of empty coal wagons. This is a return working of a power station service such as that in *Plate 115*. This train is much longer, however, with predominantly steel wagons rather than the wooden ones seen below or the mix in *Plate 118*. The steel wire fence has steel-reinforced concrete posts with intermediate metal spacers.

117 (*Opposite, middle*): The long process of shifting domestic coal started with a pick and finished with a shovel. On the S&DJR at **Shepton Mallet** in 1962, four piles of coal adorn the goods yard. The grounded clerestory coach body is MR, complete with side corridor connections. The bridge, centre left, carries the GWR branch from Witham to Wells over the S&D.

118 (*Opposite, bottom*): In 1958, a long coal train passes **Temple Mills** marshalling yard. It is headed by GER J17 class 0-6-0 No. 65528. Note the lack of vegetation on the black, shaley soil.

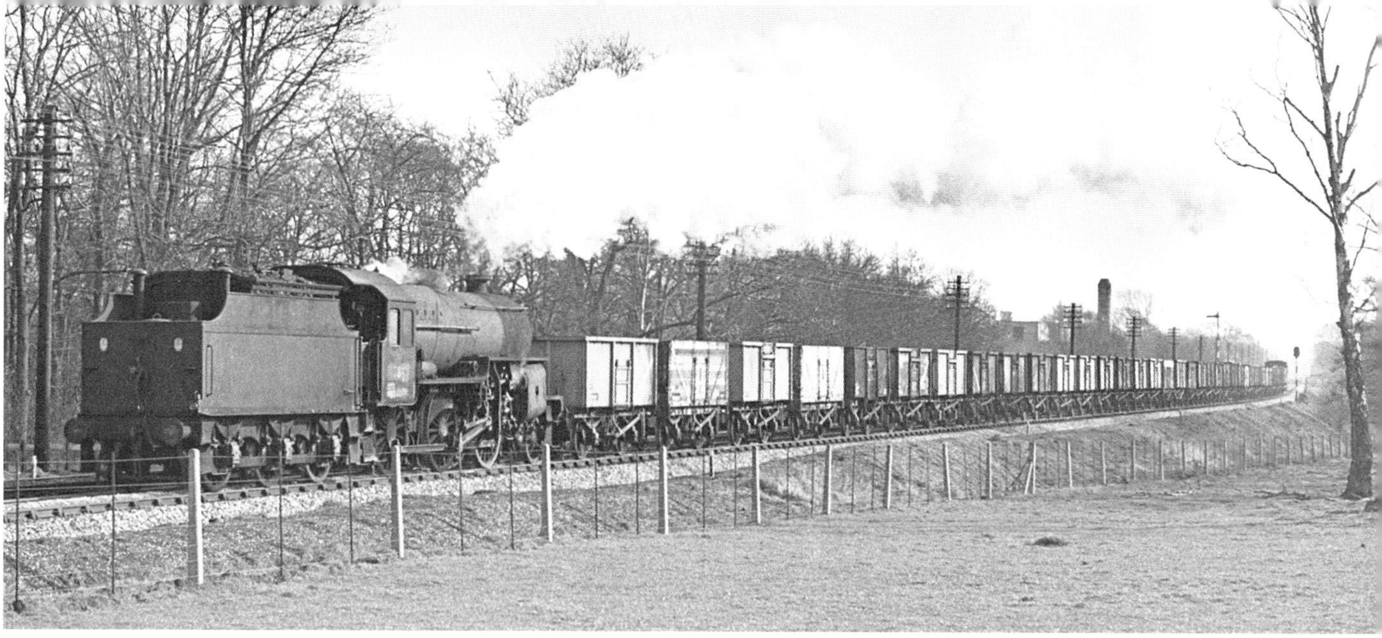

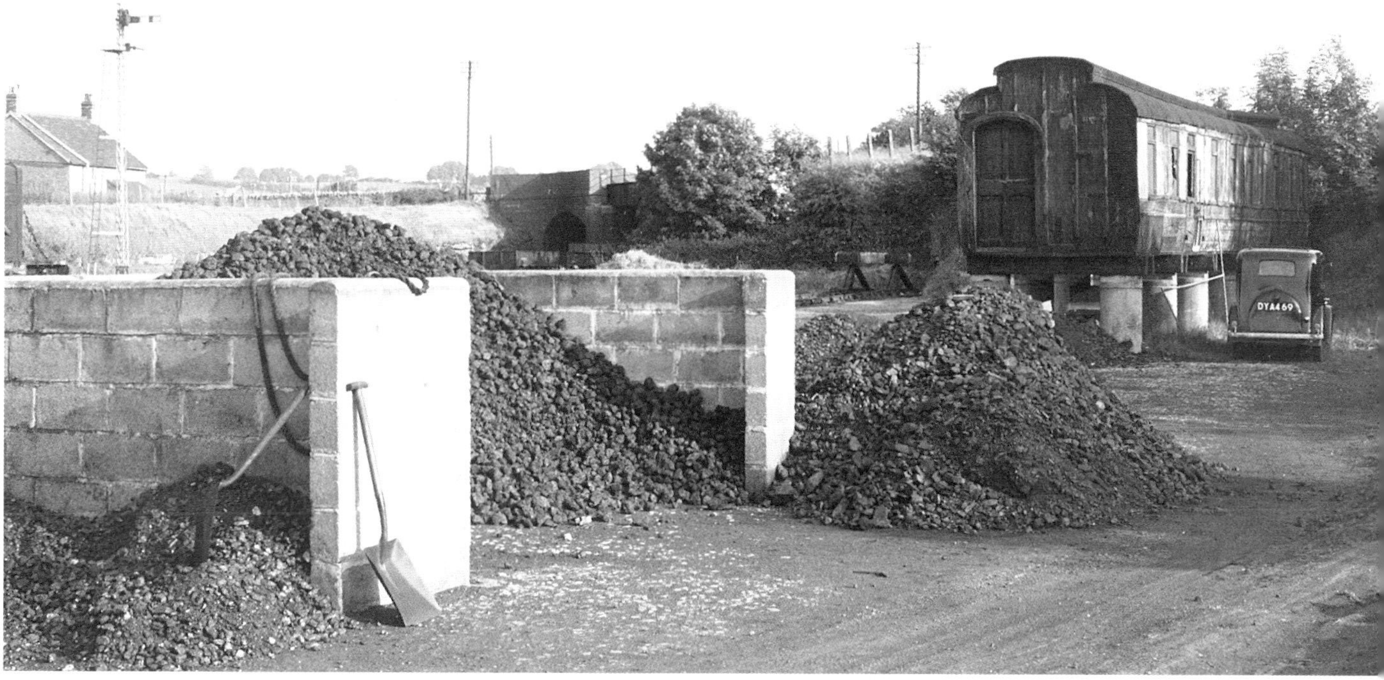
DYA469

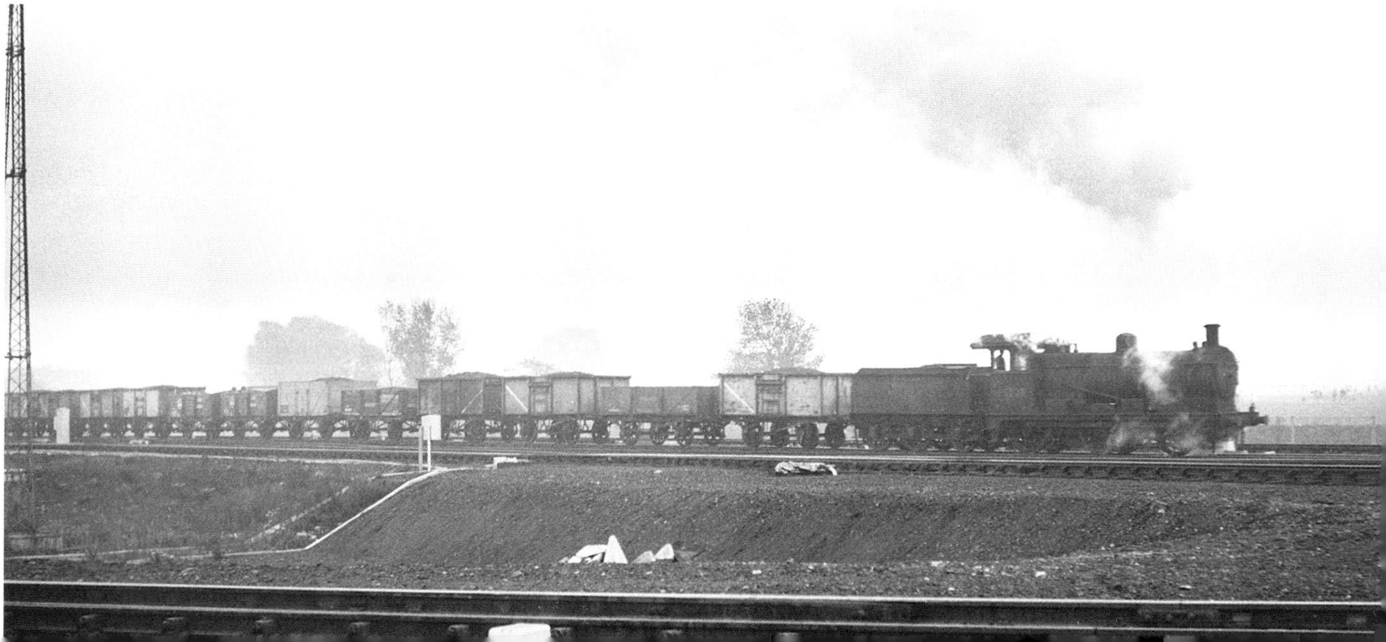

Heavy freight

119: (*Right*): In 1964, GWR Prairie tank No. 4103 passes through **Stroud** on a down freight with an interesting mix including a van, three container wagons and assorted open wagons. The platform surface is under repair in the foreground.

120 (*Below*): SR Q1 class 0-6-0 No. 33034 heads a heavy van train near **Deepdene** on the 20½-mile SER link line between Redhill and Guildford.

121 (*Opposite, top*): In 1962, LMS 'Crab' 2-6-0 No. 42939 heads a long mixed freight on the LNWR main line a few miles south-east of **Stafford**. Wagons include vans, hoppers, open trucks, tankers and cattle trucks.

122 (*Opposite, bottom*): In 1961, SR U1 class Mogul No. 31908 heads a down Continental freight on the SER main line near **Smeeth**. Car transporters can add much interest to a model railway.

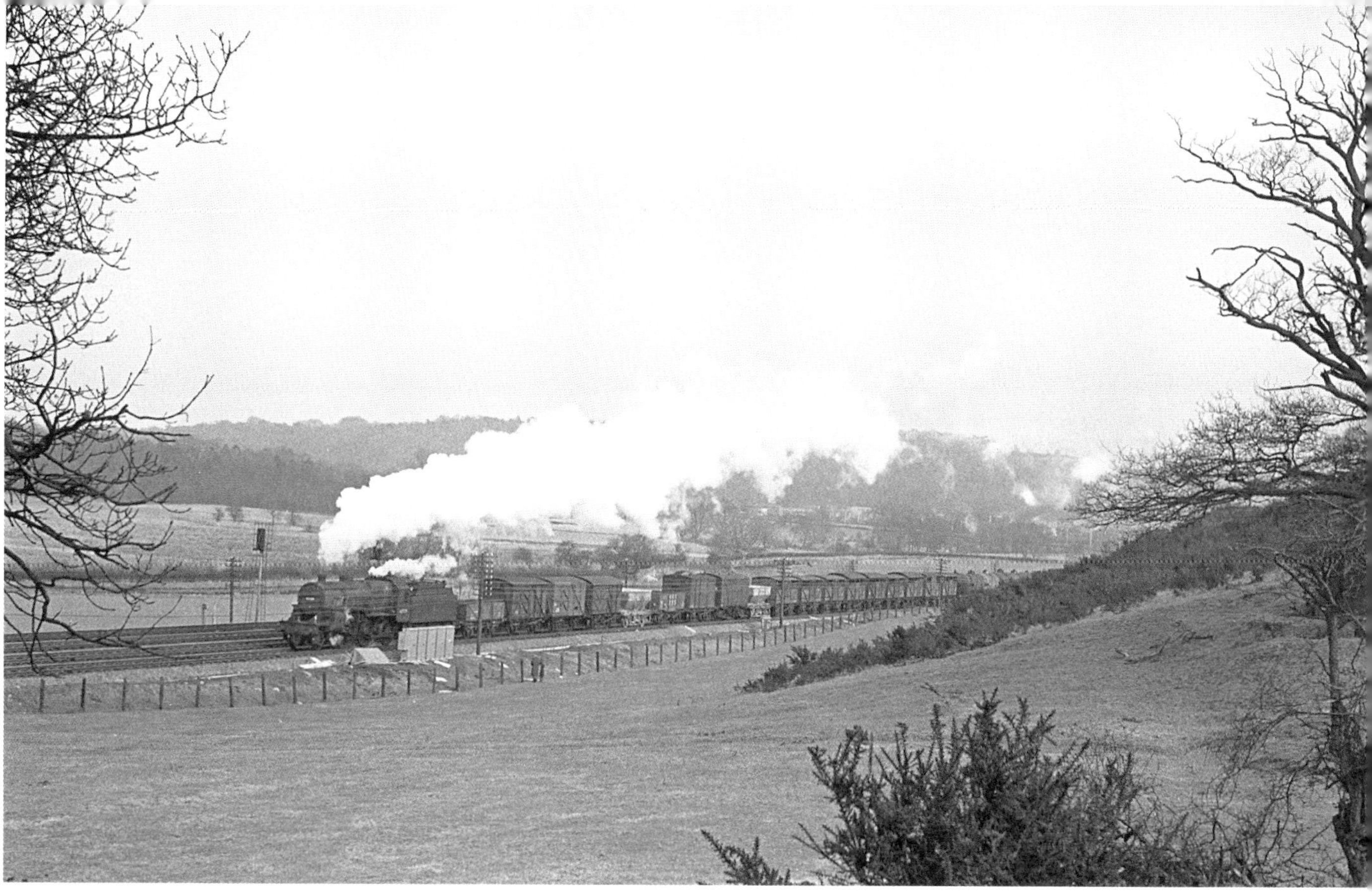

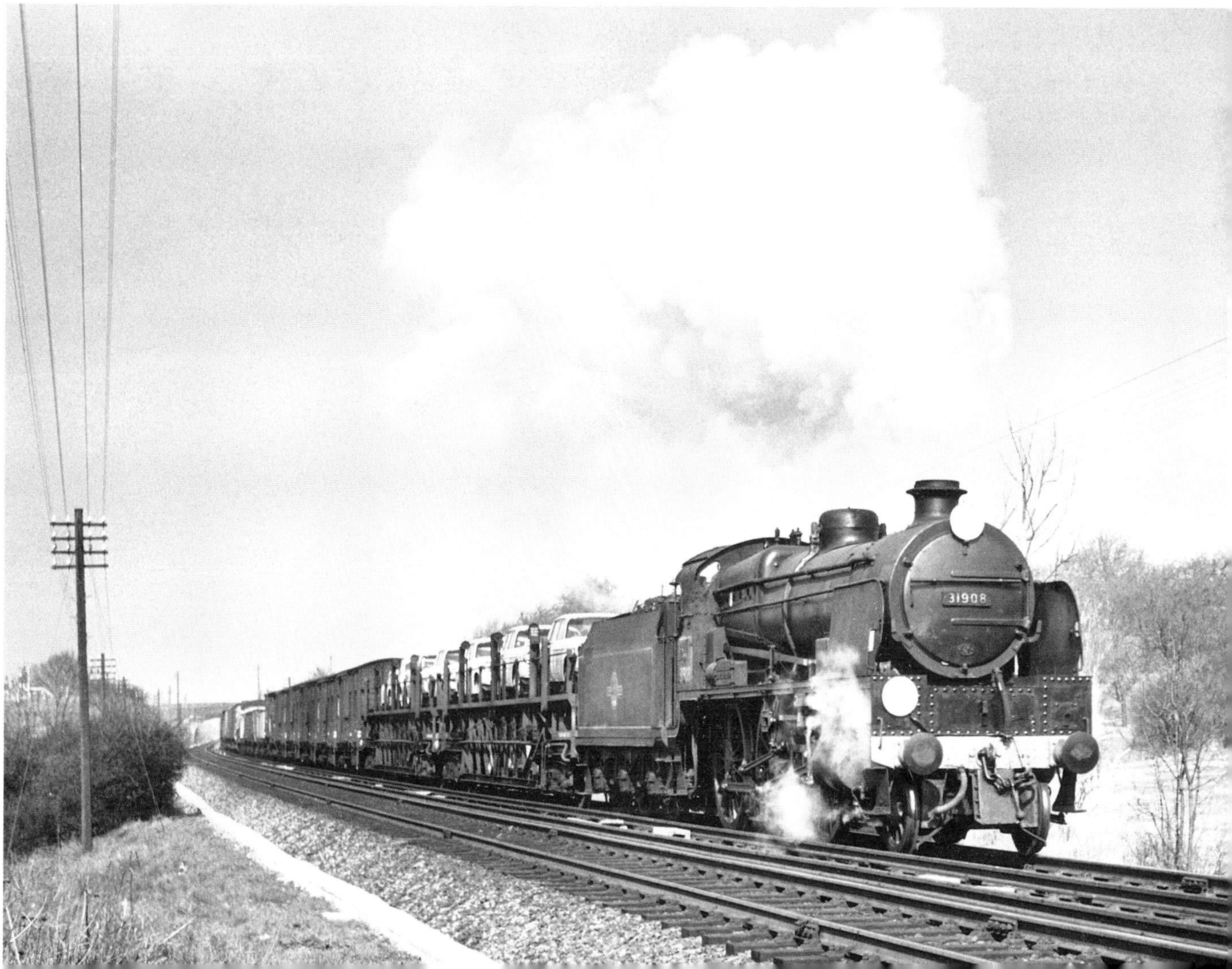
31908

Distant steam

123 N gauge layouts often feature long trains and to simulate an operator's viewpoint in full size, one needs to retreat to a far hillside. Near **Okehampton** in 1959, a Bulleid light Pacific heads a fitted freight from Plymouth.

124 A model train disappearing off-stage to a fiddle yard or a hidden loop can be most satisfying. In the late summer of 1960 at **Cranleigh**, an early morning train to Horsham is framed by trees, bushes, a telegraph pole and SR semaphore signals on an LBSCR wooden post. The level-crossing gate is already closing.

125 This N gauge simulation is on the NSR's Churnet Valley line in the Peak District near **Denstone**. In 1962, fields and a sylvan backdrop frame an LMS 2-6-4 tank with a three-coach local train to Leek.

126 Unless relieved by lineside accoutrements, four-track main lines can look bland on model railways. Here, the LNWR lineside near **Stafford** offers new OHE catenaries, colour-light signals, terminal boxes, a platelayers' hut, the telegraph, two types of fencing and a modest curvature. In 1962, the diorama was completed by LMS 'Patriot' class 4-6-0 No. 45545 *Planet* heading an up express – named but not logged.

Stopping trains

127 In 1962, GWR Mogul No. 6353 coasts towards **Shrewsbury** with a stopping train of BR Mark 1 stock from Craven Arms. The hillside creates a rural backdrop, an inclined road bridge and a low-level siding.

128 First-generation DMUs ran alongside BR steam for some 15 years. In 1962, this two-car set is approaching **Stafford** from the Wolverhampton line. The great signal brackets are LNWR (see *Plate 231*).

129 The occasional mixed train can add interest to any railway, real or model. Departing **Stalbridge** on the S&DJR in 1963, Ivatt Class 2MT 2-6-2T No. 41242 heads an unusual mix of a BR compartment-third, a corridor brake-third, a milk tank wagon and a horse box.

130 Transitions from cutting to embankment can make fine settings on model railways. This one is well endowed with scattered trees and a hilly backdrop. On the NSR near **Denstone**, in the spring of 1962, LMS Class 4MT 2-6-4T No. 42593 heads a train of LMS stock to Uttoxeter.

Trains under trees

131 In 1962, framed by winter trees in the Sow Valley, **Stafford.** The West Coast Main Line runs parallel here with the Staffordshire & Worcestershire Canal. A hump bridge over the canal can be seen just ahead of the express to Euston.

132 In 1961, just east of **Lewes**, an SR 2-BIL EMU runs between willows past the former priory of St Oswald. The distant signals are for Southerham Junction – the nearest arm is for the Seaford branch.

133 In 1960 on the MNR, a train to Ramsey stands out crystal-clear at **Kirk Michael**. On the stone wall of the goods shed, enamelled signs advertise oil engines and matches.

134 In 1962 on the NSR near **Denstone**, an LMS Class 4MT 2-6-4T runs bunker-first with a local goods train to Uttoxeter. The quiet meadows seem to glisten beneath barren winter boughs of oak and ash.

Little trains

135 (*Right*): The Stroud Valley was once served by little trains which ran to Gloucester. In 1964, a GWR small Prairie tank restarts from **Downfield Crossing Halt** with a single motor-coach while passengers walk to the ungated foot crossing. A DMU stop sign had recently been erected alongside the (empty) BR notice board, right.

136 (*Below*): Near **North Hayling** in 1958, Stroudley A1X class 0-6-0T No. 32677 heads a short train of LSWR compartment stock. This 'Terrier' entered service in 1880 as LBSCR No. 77 *Wonersh* and has the honour of being the oldest working locomotive in this book.

137 (*Top*): Near **Ford** on the outskirts of Plymouth, a GWR pannier tank is sandwiched between four push-pull auto-coaches, in 1959. These coaches have few doors, open saloons, low-back seats and good all-round visibility. They can be enjoyed today on preserved lines including the Didcot Railway Centre and South Devon Railway.

138 (*Middle*): The SR built a double-ended branch south of Torrington to light railway standards. This scene at **Watergate Halt** offers a wealth of detail including a siding, stacked sleepers, a stream underbridge and a hilly, rural backdrop. The single SR brake-third to Halwill is headed by Ivatt Class 2MT 2-6-2T No. 41295.

139 (*Bottom*): In 1963, a GWR Collett 2251 class 0-6-0 approaches **Glastonbury** from the west with two corridor coaches and a van. Much of this S&DJR branch ran on an embankment above the drains and fields of the Somerset Levels.

Transient diesels

The BR Modernisation Plan of 1955 saw no long-term future for steam. In their haste to eliminate steam, the BR Regions quickly introduced fleets of diesel locomotives. Some took over freight and passenger services on a permanent basis. Others took over certain passenger services in advance of electrification – a transient arrangement lasting anything from a few months to some years. The captions which follow give the locomotive builder, wheel arrangement, BR type and 'D' numbering as used in the early 1960s. The later BR 'TOPS' classification is given in brackets. Such 'growling' locomotives were an integral part of the 'Late Steam Age'.

140 East of Ashford near **Smeeth** in 1961, an up express from the Channel ports is piloted by BRC&W/Sulzer Bo-Bo Type 3 diesel-electric No. D6544 (later Class 33) ahead of a BR/Sulzer Bo-Bo Type 2 (later Class 24).

141 Passing hop fields near **Tonbridge** in March 1961, BR/Sulzer Bo-Bo Type 2 diesel-electric No. D5008 (later Class 24) heads an up express of Maunsell and Bulleid stock. Fifteen such diesels were on loan from LM Region until delivery of the Southern's own Type 3. Note the third rail, ready for 'E-Day'.

142 (*Right*): In 1962 at **Trentham**, English Electric 1Co-Co1 Type 4 diesel-electric No. D218 (later Class 40) heads a train from Manchester to London. The down home signals are mounted on a tall LMS tubular steel post with steadying guys. The calling-on signal has a white siting shield painted on the road bridge. The diamond indicates that track circuitry or other train detection system is installed.

143 (*Below*): At **Coventry** in February 1962, work is in progress to rebuild the station prior to installation of OHE and colour-light signalling. In the meantime, a service to Euston is headed by English Electric 1Co-Co1 Type 4 diesel-electric No. D269 (later Class 40). The platforms are littered with construction material but the LMS bracket and semaphore signals stand proud – two auxiliary arms and a starter (off).

Steam doubles

144 (*Bottom*): Double trains and locomotives can be enthralling. At **Plymouth North Road** in 1959, GWR 'Castle' class 4-6-0 No. 7006 *Lydford Castle* restarts a westbound train while another 4-6-0 approaches from a siding.

145 (*Opposite, top*): In 1962, two LMS trains cross near **Penkridge** on the LNWR, south of Stafford. The LMS 'Black Five' 4-6-0 is No. 45146, and the rear coach is a brake-third, both to the design of Sir William Stanier.

146 (*Opposite, middle*): West of **St Johns** (the only junction station on the Isle of Man), the lines to Ramsey (left) and Peel (right) ran parallel for half a mile. In 1960, 2-4-0 tanks No. 8 *Fenella* and No. 14 *Thornhill* race to the parting of the ways. The MNR line (left) was the more mountainous. Both lines are now closed.

147 (*Opposite, bottom*): In 1960 at **Ryde St Johns Road**, LSWR O2 class 0-4-4 tanks, No. 26 *Whitwell* and No. 18 *Ningwood*, run coupled together from the works. They continued to Ryde Pierhead for their next turns of duty.

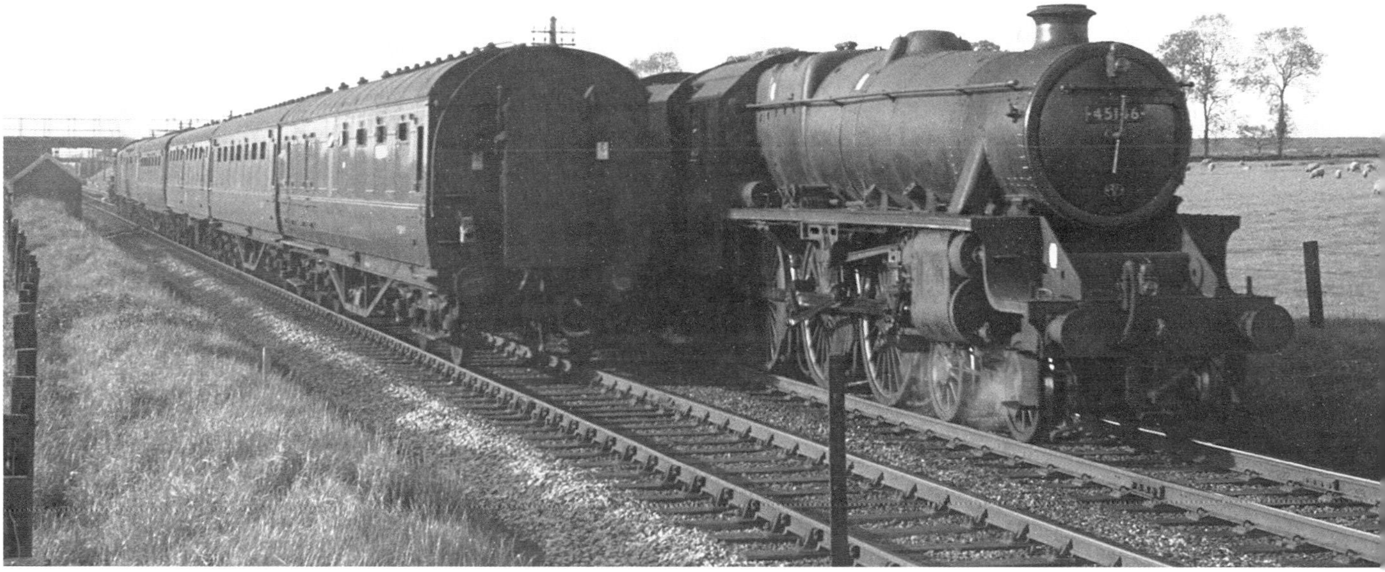

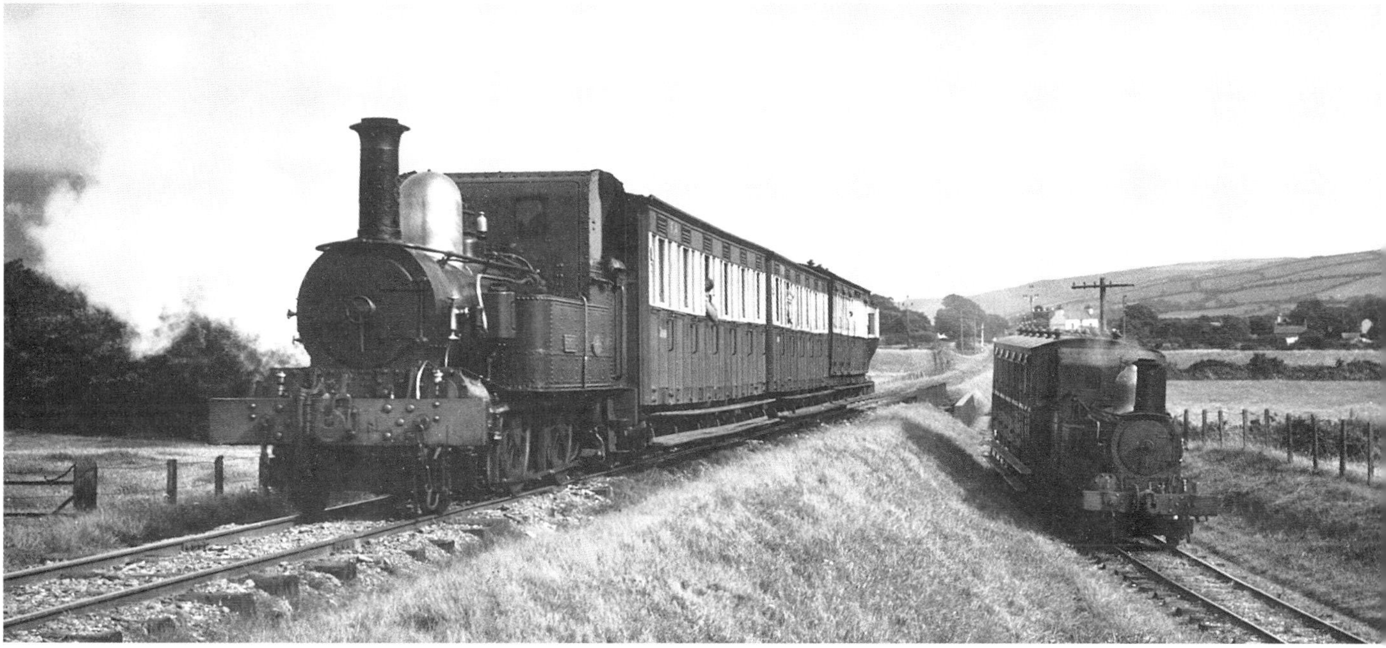

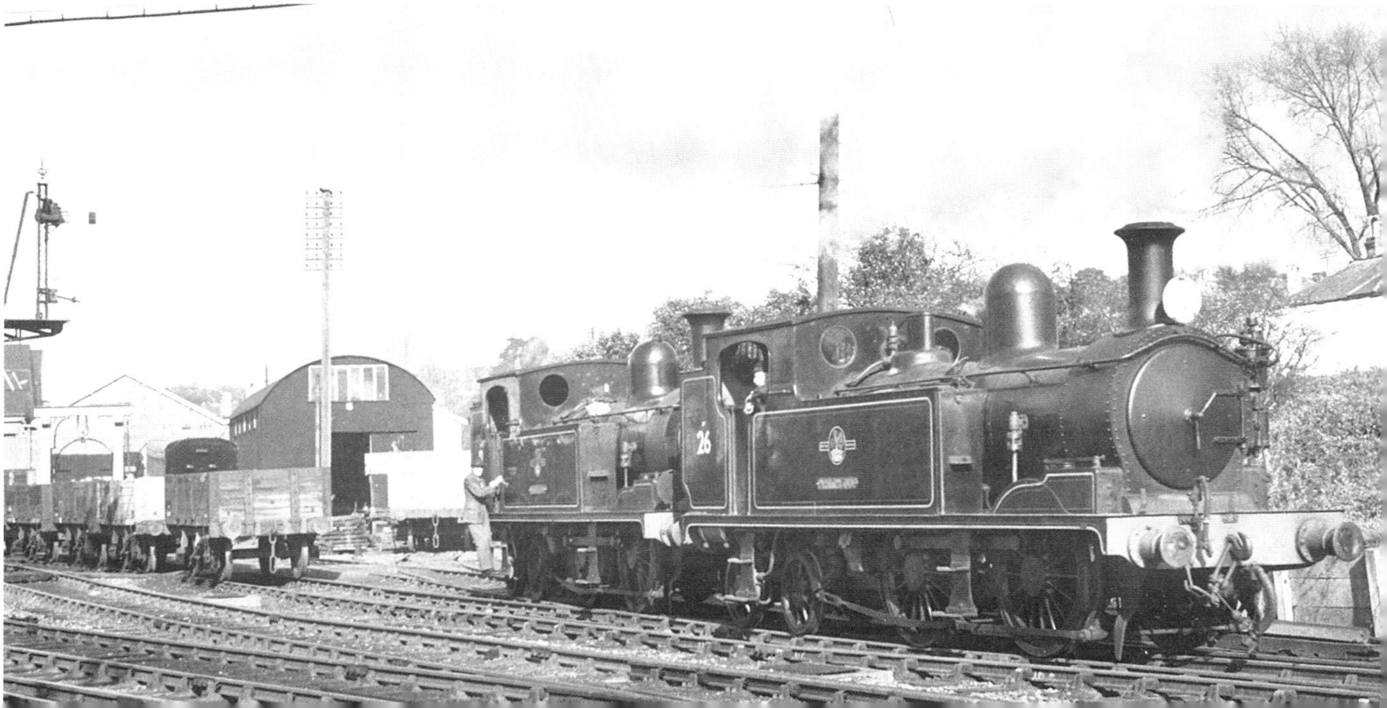
26

Urban backdrops

148 (*Right*): The backs of pubs and offices at **Holborn Viaduct** (LCDR) in 1959. Note the tallness of the buildings, the steeply pitched roofs, some ornate dormer windows at the front but plain windows overlooking the railway at the back. The grimy overhead signal box sits astride the incline down to Snow Hill station. Note the colour-light ground signals in front of three top beams of the road bridge (over Ludgate Hill).

149 (*Below*): The ends of town terraces at **Gravesend** (SER) in 1960, featuring 45° roofs, bay windows and an attached outhouse. Perhaps a million such homes were built during the Victorian era in industrial Britain. A branch train to Allhallows-on-Sea is headed by SECR H class 0-4-4T No. 31193.

150 (*Top*): The fronts of suburban terraced houses at **Herne Hill** (LCDR) in 1959 are separated from the railway by a road and a tall brick wall. These are more substantial houses than those at Gravesend (*opposite*), built for lower middle class families rather than working class. The front rail-built signal bracket is redundant and about to be demolished, replaced by the new colour-light signals. The heavy freight train approaching from the down sorting sidings is double-headed by SECR N class Mogul No. 31410 and an SR Q1 class 0-6-0.

151 (*Middle*): The backs of tall city terraced houses at **Victoria** (LCDR) in 1959 have staggered windows, projections for toilets and a multitude of chimney stacks and pots. The warehouse on the left has multi-paned windows and a fire-escape. Bulleid light Pacific No. 34085 *501 Squadron* awaits the green flag, resplendent with 'Golden Arrow' insignia and a very clean SR luggage van.

152 (*Bottom*): A plethora of commercial premises at **Waterloo (East)** (SER), viewed from the former connecting rail bridge to the LSWR station in 1959. Left to right, they include the brick premises of the Union Jack Club, the Shell building (under construction), the Gothic turrets of the old War Office (centre), a pub with ornate windows and a balustrade, the end of terraced cottages and another office block under construction (right). The train of empty stock to Charing Cross is headed by rebuilt SR light Pacific No. 34005 *Barnstaple*. Running tender-first, it will presently be released to head a later departure.

Lineside industries

153 (*Right*): Alongside the NSR main line in the Trent Valley, the chimneys of **Meaford Power Station** are brick, tapering towards the top. An inclined conveyor leads from the extensive sidings, packed with four-wheel private and BR wagons in 1962. The CEGB's 0-6-0 tank engine is Robert Stephenson & Hawthorns 7683 of 1951.

154 (*Below*): Looking east from **Southampton Central**, the LSWR running lines converge towards a semicircular tunnel portal. Coal sidings on the right lead across the road to the power station with its unusual steel chimney which tapers the wrong way for efficient dispersal of gases. Bolster and open wagons occupy the general goods yard (left). The tall concrete fence (right) is SR. In 1958, two posters advertise the Dover car ferry service – a promotion of road rather than rail travel.

155 In a bleak Dartmoor landscape near **Chilsworthy**, this mine would once have produced tin, copper and other minerals. Note the steel banding of the chimney. A white five-bar gate (centre) marks the entrance of the former PD&SWJR siding. In 1959, an Ivatt 2-6-2T heads a mixed passenger-freight train to Callington.

156 A general feature of narrow-gauge railways is their intimacy with the towns and countryside through which they pass. Near **Peel** in 1960, the IMR burrows through woodland and under a stone bridge to pass a water mill with no boundary fence. The River Neb passes beneath the foreground railway bridge.

Riverside settings

157 (*Right*): Alexandra Bridge (far right), was the LCDR's first Thames crossing at **Blackfriars**. In 1959, it was used mainly for freight and empty stock working. This north bank station was originally called St Pauls. The canopies and overall roof provide limited protection from the wind.

158 (*Bottom*): The LSWR branch to Turnchapel and the GWR branch to Yealmpton shared the **Laira** bridge over the River Plym. Both branches had closed to passengers by 1959. Trundling across with a freight train from Plymouth is Drewry 0-6-0 diesel shunter (later Class 04) No. 11225.

159 (*Opposite, top*): Massive cast-iron piers support Sir John Hawkshaw's bridge over the Thames to **Cannon Street** (SER). He also designed the single-arch station roofs at both Charing Cross and Cannon Street. The former collapsed in 1905 and the latter was severely damaged by bombs during the Second World War. In 1958, work was in progress to dismantle the roof at Cannon Street. The twin towers were ornamental.

160 (*Opposite, bottom*): For about two miles, the GER line between **Haddiscoe** and Reedham runs on an embankment of the New Cut (a canal connecting the rivers Waveney and Yar). In 1959, GNR K3 class Mogul No. 61926 shunts near this level crossing/drawbridge combination. To hand-crank the bridge, the St Olaves signalman (*Plate 247*) would cycle several hundred yards to join the crossing keeper, working one on either side.

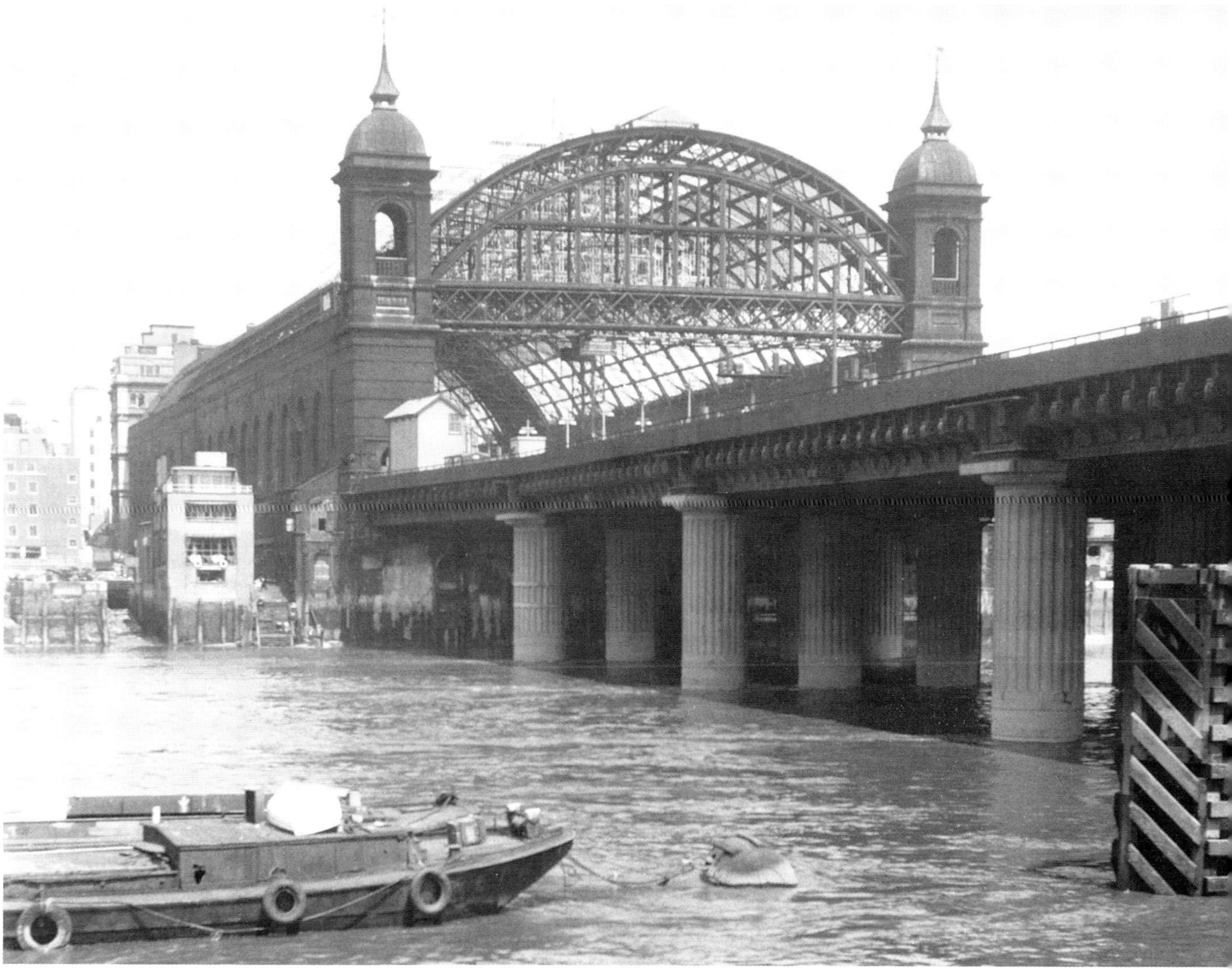

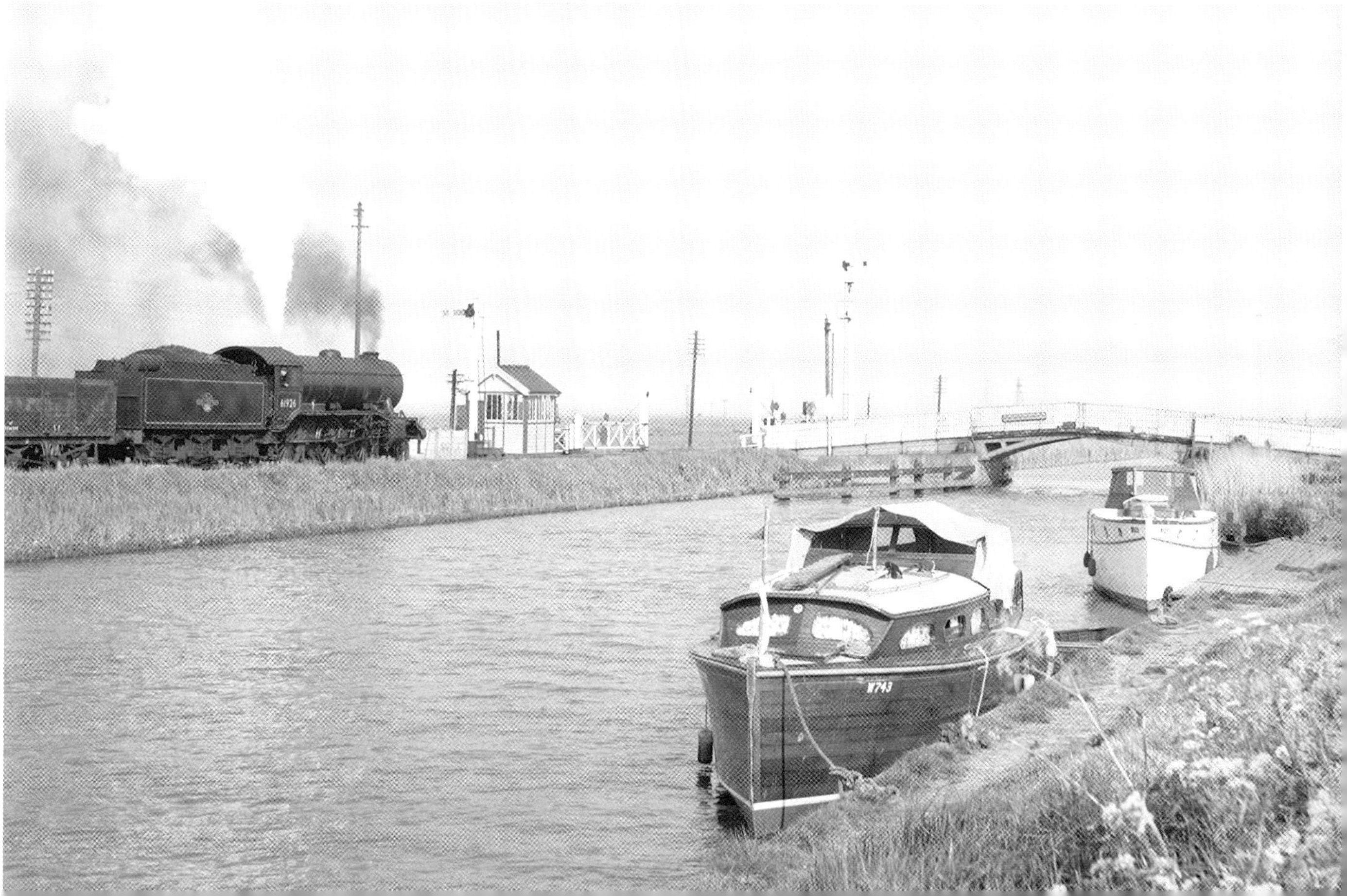
W743

Steel bridges

161 The high-level section of **Portsmouth & Southsea** station was built on a steel viaduct. The sides are steel (for strength) but the island platform is timber (for lightness). In 1958, an EMU from Brighton climbs the incline and a train of 4-COR units stands in the cleaning sidings (right). The low-level terminus is on the left.

162 The 1959 RCTS railtour from Liverpool Street (*Plate 2*) reversed at **East Finchley** on the Northern Line before running via the Widened Lines to North Kent. Fitted with condensing pipes into its side-tanks, GNR N2 class 0-6-2T No. 69504 prepares to restart the train of Gresley stock. The road bridge has massive riveted girders with a central support. Note how the top plate is thicker in mid-span where the stress is greatest. This GNR station was rebuilt by LT in the elegant 'modern' style of the inter-war years.

163 Whereas flat steel bridges usually incorporate vertical sides for strength and rigidity, arched bridges achieve rigidity by compression of the arch. At **East Dulwich**, the tops of the arch protrude between the rails, requiring a break in the electric conductor rail to avoid short-circuiting. Two clean 4-SUB units cross in 1960 with No. 4679 approaching.

164 North of Plymouth, **Tamerton Creek** is crossed on a steel viaduct with protruding central reinforcing girders. In 1959, a short train of Maunsell stock is headed by an LSWR M7 class 0-4-4 tank.

Brick bridges

165 Near **Chilham** on the SER line to Canterbury West, this five-arch low bridge allows free drainage into the Great Stour and seasonal overflow back onto the flood plain. In 1961, a local passenger service to Ashford is headed by a Bo-Bo diesel-electric locomotive on loan from LM Region (see *Plates 140* to *143*).

166 This long arch bridge (or short tunnel) at **Gravesend** (SER) carries a road junction. It has a roof arc of about 60°. In 1960, SECR H class 0-4-4T No. 31322 propels a push-pull set towards Allhallows.

167 One of the oldest railway bridges in Britain is near **Whitstable Town** on the Canterbury & Whitstable line. It is narrow with a full 180° arc. Opened in 1830, the C&WR was absorbed by the SER in 1853.

168 Rectangular bridge apertures are useful space-savers on model railways. Those at **Eridge** have brick columns and parapets but the beams are of steel and concrete. They support a road and the LBSCR station building. In 1959, BR Standard Class 4MT 2-6-4T No. 80147 restarts from the down island platform with a train to Eastbourne.

Tunnel approaches

169 (*Below, left*): Curvature of the line obscures the portal, but bare chalk marks the south entrance to **Polhill Tunnel** on the SER main line. In 1960, a rebuilt Bulleid light Pacific approaches with an up express. On the right is a Whistle sign, the electric substation, a signal bracket and the telegraph is either side of the line.

170 (*Below, right*): The S&DJR was originally single-track through **Windsor Hill Tunnel.** When this section of the line was doubled, a second single-track tunnel was bored, resulting in this unusual northern approach, bisected by the signal box and a platelayers' hut. Mendip limestone shows through the rich vegetation in 1962.

171 (*Opposite, top*): In 1865, to serve the Great Exhibition, the LCDR built a branch to **Crystal Palace (High Level)**. In 1963, nine years after line closure, the grandeur of the site can still be appreciated from the tunnel. The cutting wall, with its buttresses and alcoves, can make an attractive backdrop on a model railway.

172 (*Opposite, bottom*): On the northern section of the LBSCR's Bluebell line, **West Hoathley Tunnel** has a classic elliptical shape. The portal and abutments are nicely finished in brick, but not too elaborate. A platelayers' hut is generally to be found at either end of a long tunnel. New tree growth was apparent in 1959.

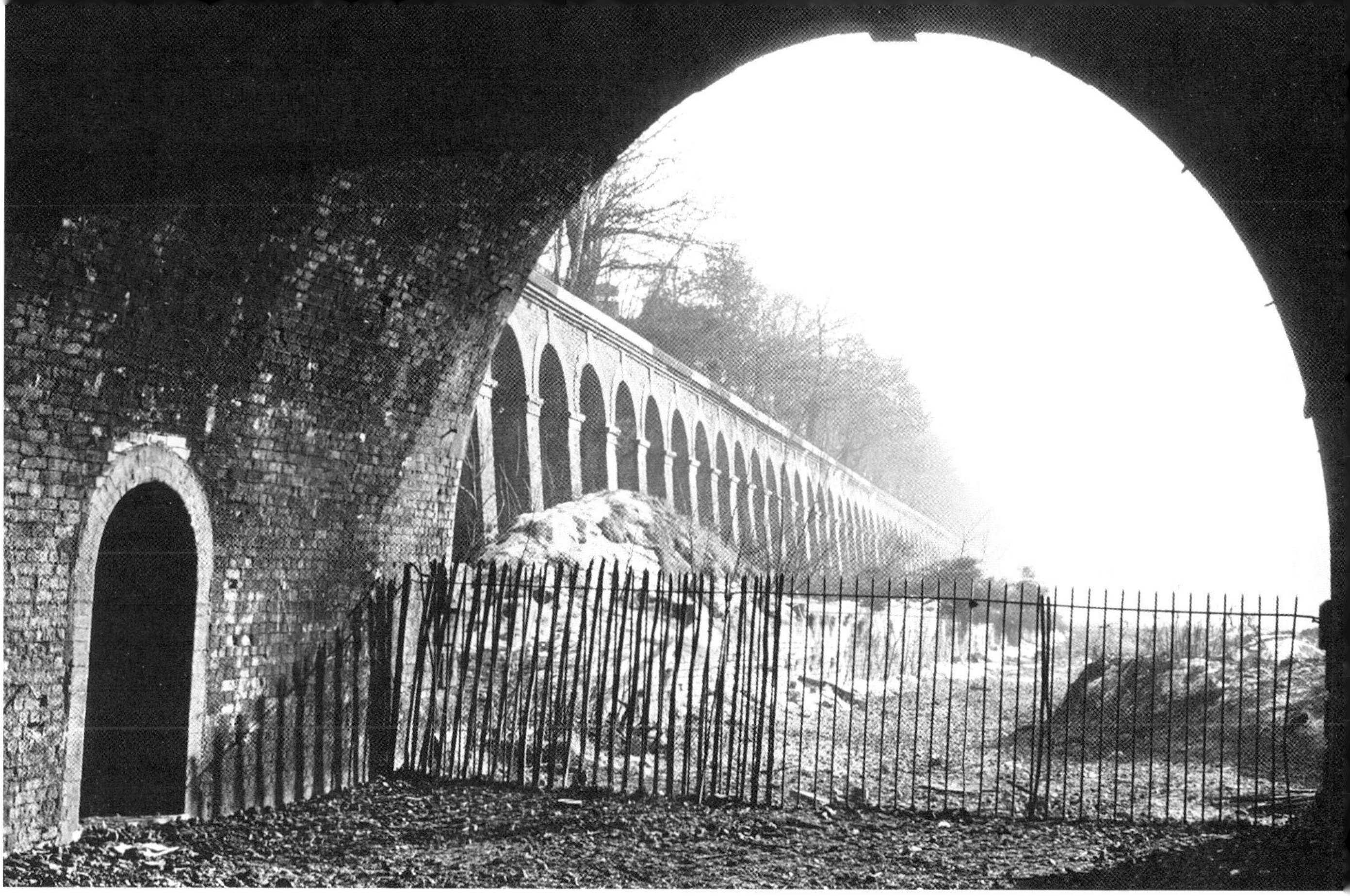

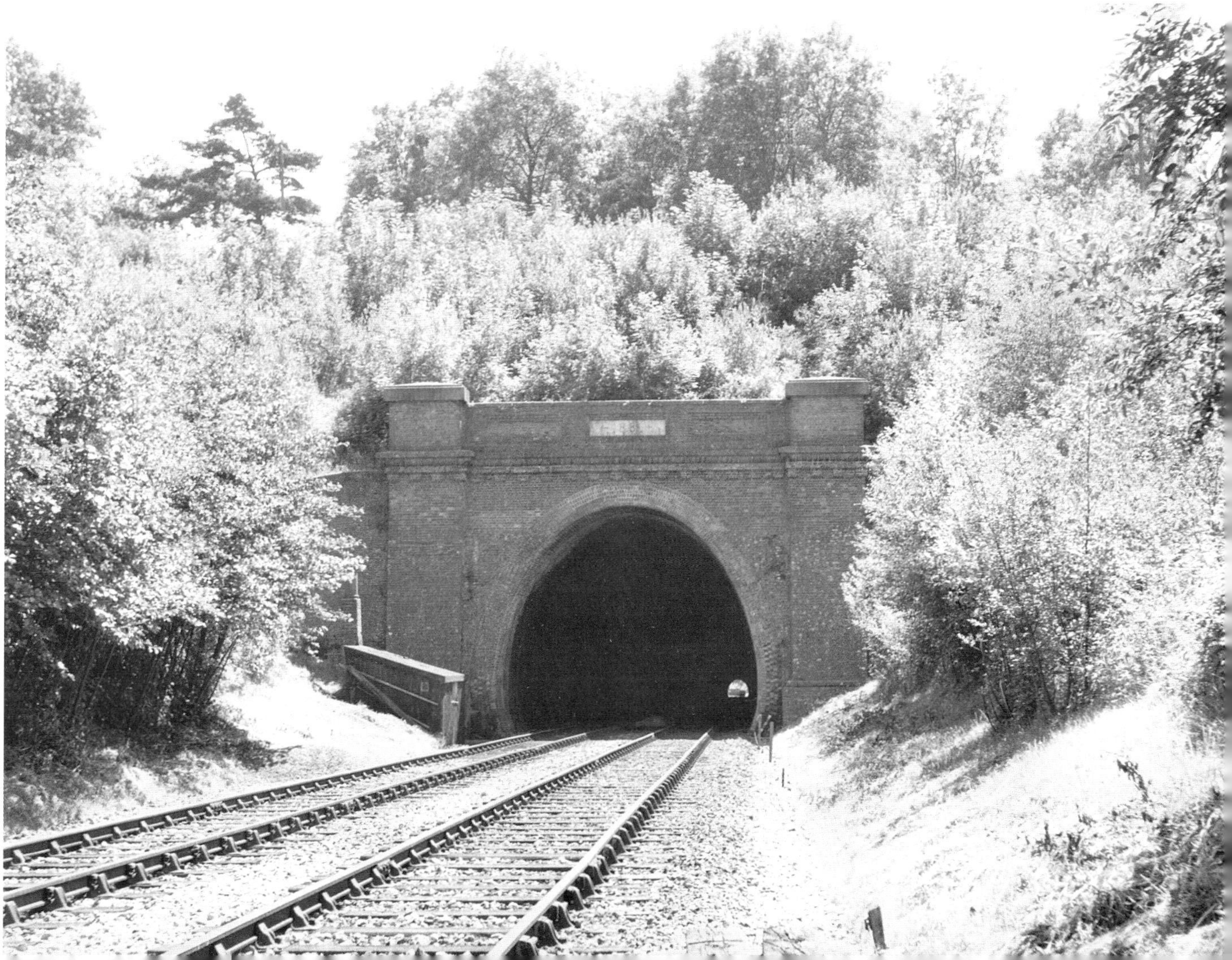

Cutting angles

173 The LBSCR liked to create flat sites for stations by cutting into the hillside and dumping the spoil on the other (lower) side. Such is the case at **Cowden** on the approach to Markbeech Tunnel. The open space was ideal for photography and was available for development. In 1964, Ivatt Class 2MT 2-6-2T No. 41260 heads a short train from Oxted. The conifers and silver birch are magnificent.

174 Chalk is more stable than clay. On the EKR near **Shepherds Well**, this cutting has a 60° angle to the horizontal. Too steep for much grass to grow, there are fallen pieces of chalk crumble on both sides. The thin topsoil is also evident. This line was independent until 1948, and in 1961 it served just Tilmanstone Colliery.

175 The cutting at **Ore** (through unstable Hastings beds) is shallow-angled at about 25° to the horizontal. There are several hollows where minor slippages have occurred after wet weather. In 1961, BR Standard Class 4MT 2-6-4T No. 80041 heads a set of BR Mark 1 stock towards Ashford. To its left are the cooling tower pond and main building of the closed Hastings (steam) power station. Such wide cuttings are rare on model railways.

176 In 1962, BR Standard Class 3MT 2-6-2T No. 82005 heads a four-coach stopping train on the GWR/LNWR joint line south of **Shrewsbury**. The cutting has an angle of 45° and is neatly lined with hedges.

Embankments

177 Most embankments are angled at about 45°. This curved one on the GWR branch near **Shepton Mallet High Street** is sprinkled with summer flowers and emerges from a cutting (also at about 45°). In 1962, BR Standard Class 3MT 2-6-2T No. 82007 heads a two-coach local of GWR and BR stock towards Witham.

178 To avoid domination on model railways, embankments are best kept short. On the IWR near **Wroxall**, scrub and a farm bridge add visual relief to this steep embankment (at about 60° to the horizontal). In 1960, LSWR O2 class 0-4-4T No. 27 *Merstone* heads an up five-coacher of SECR and LBSCR stock.

179 Battledown flyover carries up Southampton trains over the LSWR West of England main line (foreground) via two long inclined embankments. In 1963, Bulleid light Pacific No. 34103 *Calstock* brings an up 13-coacher of BR Mark 1 stock down the incline towards Worting Junction. Note the massive telegraph and the unusual combination of a steel bridge under the foreground lines and a brick tunnel through the embankment.

180 Near **Peel Road Halt** on the bleak west coast of Man, this embankment echoes the steep angle of the hillside beyond. In 1960, Beyer Peacock 2-4-0 tank No. 8 *Fenella* heads a mixed train towards Ramsey. The open wagon on the rear would have been gravity-shunted into a siding at one of the intermediate stations.

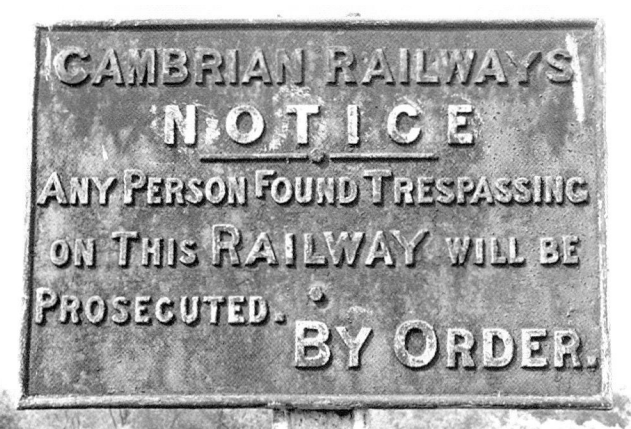

Cast-iron signs

181 (*Above*): The message is clear and simple on this CR trespass sign on the Llanfyllin branch near **Llanymynech**. Seen in 1962, mounted on bullhead rail.

182 (*Right*): The small print is barely legible on this neglected trespass sign on the GNR's Stafford branch at **Salt**. Dated 1898 and mounted on a ferro-concrete fence post, it may have been damaged during remounting to cause a crack through the bolt holes. Pictured in 1962.

183 (*Below*): Although damaged and flaked with surface rust, the message remains clear on this NSR bridge load sign near **Meaford Power Station**. Less clear is what is meant by 'Ordinary traffic of the district'. Hay wains, perhaps? It was carried on a wooden post in 1962.

184 (*Above*): For clarity, the letters have been carefully painted white on this trespass sign at the GCR/GWR joint station at **High Wycombe**. Although cast with corner holes, two extra holes have been drilled for mounting on a bullhead rail post. Photographed in 1962.

185 (*Top, right*): Dark letters are painted roughly but clearly on this LNWR foot crossing sign on the Wellington line near **Stafford**. Mounted on a steel post, one bolt head was broken off in 1962.

186 (*Bottom*): In 1962, letters are white on this GWR private path notice on the CR at **Four Crosses**. To avoid the central cracking problem seen in *Plate 182*, the sign was fixed to a wooden board before bolting to the bullhead rail.

187 (*Right*): A well-maintained GWR & MR trespass sign at **Shepton Mallet High Street**. New bolt holes have been drilled for mounting on a wooden post. The letters are neatly painted in white but the message is lost in legal verbosity. Unusually for 1962, full pre-Grouping ownership is painted. This is a misnomer, however, since the Midland was never a party to this line.

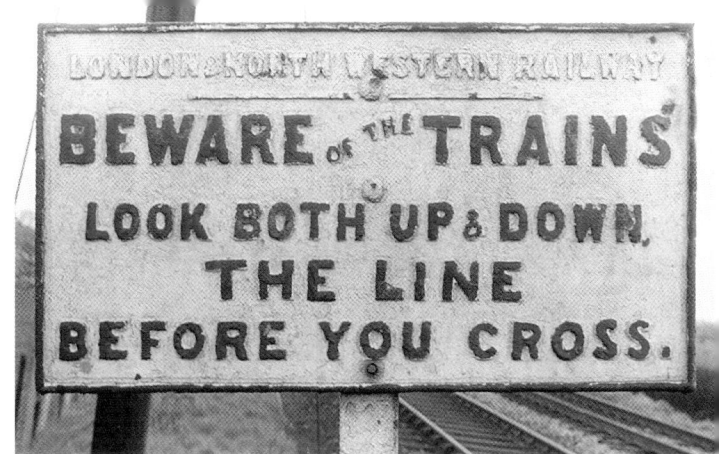

Point levers

188 (*Right*): When a point is connected to a running line, a plunger is generally provided to lock the blades in position. On the Nene Valley line at **Barnwell**, this outside ground frame has two LNWR levers – one for point operation and one for the plunger. The frame is mounted on timber baulks. See *Plate 82* for a locking mechanism and *Plate 267* for a second ground frame at this station. In 1963, LNER B1 class 4-6-0 No. 61059 restarts with a local train from Peterborough.

189 (*Below*): On the SER's Westerham branch at **Brasted**, this short weighted point lever operates in a vertical plane through almost 180°. The sleepers look fairly new, so the lever may not be an original.

190 (*Left*): In 1958, this LSWR ground frame guarded the level crossing on the LBSCR's Hayling Island branch at **Langston**. The refuge hut is an early form of signal box.

191 (*Below*): This unweighted lever at **Brasted** is much longer than that in *Plate 189,* operating through about 90°. The two types of lever were common throughout Britain. Each is painted white and pivots in a casting bolted to a pair of extended wooden sleepers. Some had a guard railing alongside as seen in *Plate 300*. The sleepers are decaying visibly, suggesting that they and this lever may be originals. The station was 80 years old when photographed in 1961.

Level crossings

192 (*Right*): A level-crossing keeper's cottage on the SER line between Ramsgate Town and **Margate Sands**. Opened in 1846, the line closed in 1926 as part of the SR's rationalisation of Isle of Thanet services. It became a footpath and a haven for wildlife (see *Plate 206*). The concrete blocks would have been added early during the Second World War to impede German armour in case of invasion.

193 (*Below*): A farm gate and public wicket gate on the NSR line north of **Uttoxeter**. In 1962, LMS Class 4MT 2-6-4T No. 42663 heads a mixed goods train of hoppers and vans.

194 A crossing at **Baynards** on the Horsham to Guildford branch. In 1960, the SR gates had X bracing, wire meshing and central red circles. The signal box is an LBSCR Type 3b. The neat station building has tall chimneys, elaborate tiling, a near-end extension and an arc-roof canopy with a late-LBSCR loping valance.

195 The IWCR line from Newport to Sandown closed in 1956 and was lifted in 1960 – a sad sight. The level crossing gates at **Alverstone** had a mix of X and N bracing. The station house is a replacement built in the early 1900s. Its suburban charm derives from the rendering, large gable window and neat tiling.

The telegraph

196 (*Right*): Trunk railway lines were used for carrying both railway and non-railway telegraph services, generally single-wire with earth return. In 1961, the LSWR's **Clapham** cutting had three rows of poles. Those on the up side, seen here, carried 96 lines on 24 spars. The skew bridge has an attractive combination of brick arches for the outer tracks and steel beams for the central pair.

197 (*Below*): The LSWR at **St Denys** had 13 spars on the down poles and 12 on the up. In 1959, a Southampton boat train is headed by SR light Pacific No. 34006 *Bude*. The lamp, its standard and the nameboard are SR. Note the brick step for staff to cross the line. For modelling, the three-storey mansions make a fine backdrop in half-relief.

198 Telegraph wires were often strung between platform lamp standards. Such is the case at **Eastleigh**, featuring SR art-deco standards. In 1961, a Western Region DMU occupies the up platform while a bunch of spotters inspect GWR 'Hall' class 4-6-0 No. 6930 *Aldersey Hall*. The great footbridge looks LSWR vintage.

199 In a richly wooded valley on the SR branch south of **Torrington**, the telegraph comprised a mere three wires on a single spar. In 1959, an Ivatt Class 2MT 2-6-2T heads a mixed train of a goods van, open wagon, steel mineral wagon, Maunsell brake-third and an SR goods brake. It was a far cry from Waterloo!

Lineside huts

200 (*Right*): In 1963, springs and debris are piled outside this tall ridged hut on the GWR line near **Basingstoke**.

201 (*Below*): On the SER's Hawkhurst branch, three huts stand alongside the up facing point at **Cranbrook**. Left to right, they are for platelayers, a trolley and coal. In 1959, SECR H class 0-4-4T No. 31266 propels a push-pull set.

202 (*Opposite, top*): On the MR near **Ketton and Collyweston**, this smart wooden hut has a stovepipe chimney. In 1963, a mixed goods train is headed by LMS 'Black Five' 4-6-0 No. 44811. The wooden fencing is MR style.

203 (*Opposite, middle*): This trolley hut at **Evercreech New** has a grindstone alongside. In 1962, BR Standard Class 4MT 4-6-0 No. 75073 heads a train to Bournemouth. The modest stone building is in a cottage style with a cantilevered canopy to the platform edge. The rail-built signal post and finial are S&DJR.

204 (*Opposite, bottom*): This hut on the LSWR main line near **Whitchurch North** has a brick chimney. In 1963, BR Standard Class 5MT 4-6-0 No. 73088 *Joyous Gard* heads two SR parcels vans and a three-coach Bulleid set.

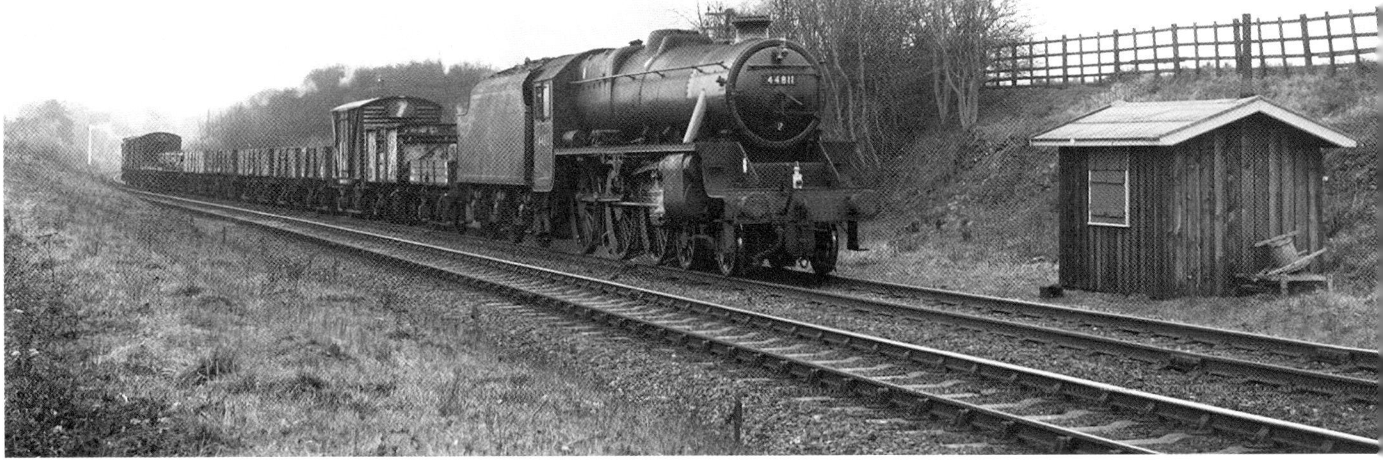
44811

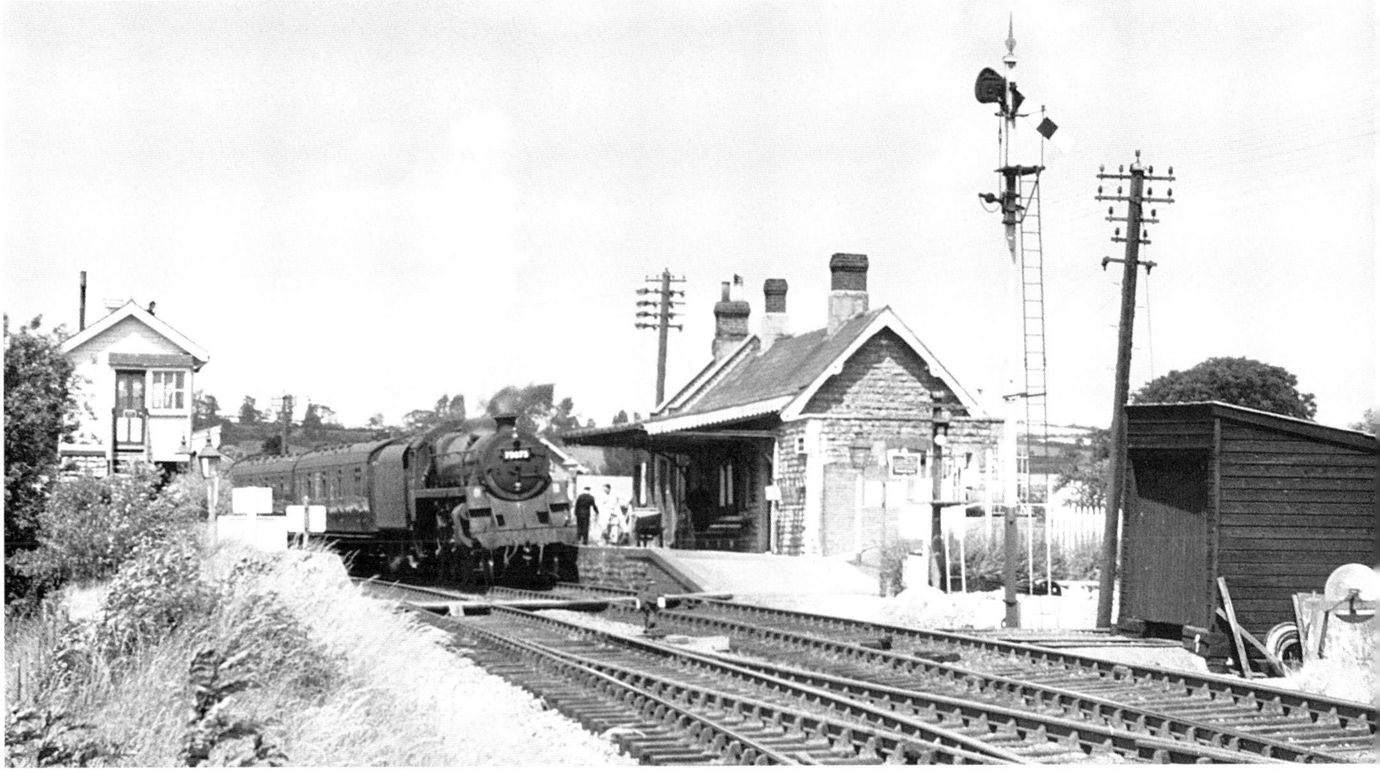

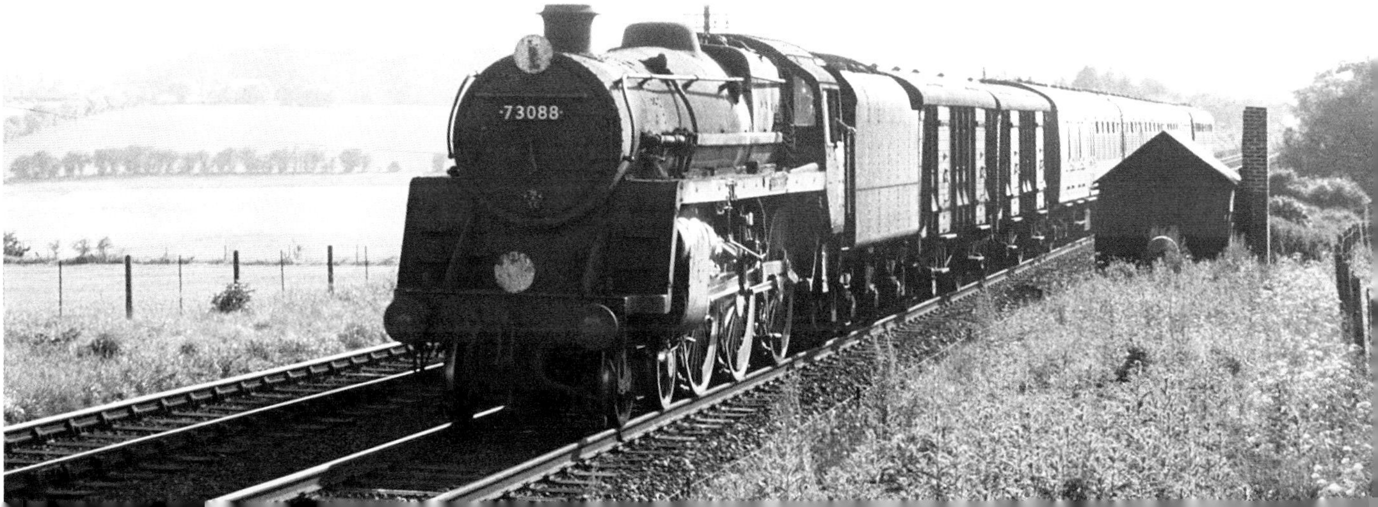
73088

Jungle encroachment

205 (*Above*): In a pastoral Montgomeryshire setting, the preserved CR narrow-gauge Welshpool & Llanfair Light Railway runs through grass and shrubs near **Castle Caereinion**. In 1962, a Whitsun Holiday train is headed by Beyer Peacock 0-6-0T No. 1 *The Earl*.

206 (*Left*): Following the SR's rationalisation of Thanet in 1926, the SER's **Margate Sands** line was abandoned except for a mile or so of siding at the Margate end. In 1959, the buffer stop is engulfed in thick undergrowth, beneath the camera position. Only the telegraph survived. See also *Plate 192*.

207 (*Left*): The GER had two branch lines which terminated at Maldon East. On the southbound branch (the first to close), **Maldon West** was the first station. In 1963, the encroaching undergrowth is well established. The station building is located alongside the road bridge to create a short tunnel. A lone passenger waits in vain for the next train to Woodham Ferrers.

208 (*Below*): The GNR owned a remote, little-used branch between Stafford and Uttoxeter. It connected via the NSR to the GNR line at Eggington and on to Derby, Nottingham and Grantham. In 1962, trees, gorse and other shrubs engulf **Weston** station in the Trent Valley. The McK&H Type 2 signal box is leaning noticeably.

Surprise encounters

209 (*Right*): The **Weymouth Harbour Tramway** was jointly owned by the GWR and LSWR. In 1963, GWR 5700 class 0-6-0 pannier tank No. 7782 shares the public road with a No. 61B 'low-bridge' bus.

210 (*Below*): This boiler and well wagon at **Southampton Docks** make a neat combination for modelling. The boiler was en route in 1958 from Eastleigh Works via Medina Wharf to Ryde for one of the Isle of Wight's LSWR O2 class 0-4-4 tanks.

211 (*Opposite, top*): High on the cliffs of the west coast of Man, 'leaves on the line' were never a problem but goats were another matter. In 1960, this herd is tethered near the distant signal of **St Germaines** (MNR). For ease of walking and grazing, the sleepers are overlaid with ballast – a practice which can accelerate rotting.

212 (*Opposite, middle*): On the GWR's Reading to Basingstoke line, this two-car EMU of pre-1938 LT tube stock was spotted in 1963 at **Bramley**. Repainted with War Department numbering, its destination was unknown.

213 (*Opposite, bottom*): Restored by LT in Metropolitan maroon livery, Class A 4-4-0 condensing tank No. 23 arrives at **Clapham Transport Museum** (behind the camera) in 1961. Built by Beyer Peacock in 1866, it worked in central London until electrification in 1905. It then worked on outer London services until 1948, latterly for shunting and engineers' trains (*Ref. 6*). Today, it can be found in London's Transport Museum at Covent Garden.

A. Masters
ART WALLPAPERS
WALLPAPERS
PICKFORDS
PICKFORDS
23
M1826

Wooden signal posts

214 (*Below*): This tapered wooden up starter signal arm at **Horsted Keynes** is LBSCR, together with its square wooden post. In 1959, the station was still BR-owned with an electrified rail connection to Haywards Heath. Today, the station is preserved as part of the Bluebell Railway.

215 (*Opposite, top*): Near **Maldon**, Essex, this lower quadrant home signal is mounted on a GER square wooden post. In 1963, together with a GER cast-iron trespass sign, it frames a two-car Metro-Cammell DMU.

216 (*Opposite, bottom*): On the Isle of Man at **St Johns**, two wooden home signals are mounted in tandem on a square wooden post. They guard the lines to Peel (left) and to Ramsey (right). The signal arms and the signal box windows resemble those at Llanfyllin (*Plate 218*), indicating that Dutton was the common contractor.

217 (*Left*): This tapered wooden GWR post is on the Wells branch near **Cranmore**. It carries a faded fixed-distant wooden arm and an oil lamp.

218 (*Below*): At **Llanfyllin**, this wooden starter and its post were installed by Dutton & Co. Ltd, signal contractor to the CR. The platelayers' hut looks modern, sturdily built of brick with a concrete roof. Ivatt Mogul No. 46519 can be seen shunting in 1962.

Rail-built and lattice posts

219 (*Right*): In 1959 at **Selsdon** (joint SER/LBSCR), a short, SR rail-built post with SER-type cap finial carries a flat stop arm and a fluted distant arm. Note also the guard rail, ballast bin, fogman's hut and a detonator lever.

220 (*Below, left*): At **Shepton Mallet Charlton Road** (S&DJR), this tall lattice post of LSWR design has three steadying guys. In 1962, BR Standard 9F class 2-10-0 No. 92001 heads a down train.

221 (*Below, right*): In 1958 at **Langston** (LBSCR), a single lattice post carries both the down home and the Havant fixed distant. The post and finial are of LSWR/SR design.

222 (*Above*): Near **Shepton Mallet Charlton Road**, an S&DJR rail-built post with conical cast finial carries the up (northbound) distant arm. In 1962, BR Standard 9F class 2-10-0 No. 92233 heads a train to Bournemouth.

223 (*Left*): In 1964 at **Selling**, an LCDR lattice post and 'spade' finial carries an SR starting arm. The concrete platelayers' hut and enamelled sign are both SR.

224 (*Below*): A pair of lattice posts with a white siting shield for improved visibility of the **West Moors** up home. In 1963, SR N class Mogul No. 31814 heads a down train.

Tubular signal posts

225 (*Right*): South of **Stafford** in 1962, a three-car DMU heads towards Wolverhampton. New colour-light signals are mounted on a tubular steel post but are not yet in commission. Mesh guards prevent maintenance workers from reaching towards OHE cables (soon to be installed).

226 (*Below*): In 1959 at **Denmark Hill**, new colour-light signals are ready to be commissioned on the LCDR's Catford Loop line. This four-aspect set is mounted on a tubular steel post alongside construction debris and a new telephone box. The old SR semaphores are nearer the tunnel and there is a banner repeater on the up line. On the far side is an SR substation, no doubt built in the 1920s for line electrification. The LBSCR signal box on the right is a relic of the South London line.

227 Early exponents of tubular signal posts were the LMS and GWR. **Condover** is a closed station on the GWR/LNWR joint line south of Shrewsbury. In 1962, this GWR home signal stood in an idyllic setting with a platelayers' hut, siding, signal box, over-bridge, the trunk telegraph and a row of wind-bent pines.

228 In 1967 at **Inverness**, the signal posts were LMS tubular (foreground) and HR lattice. The two auxiliary signals are Warning (left) for something unsighted, and Calling-on (right) for light engines. The BRC&W/Sulzer Bo-Bo Type 2 diesel-electric locomotive (later Class 26) No. D5346 is fitted with snow ploughs.

Signal brackets

229 (*Right*): A signal bracket is defined as having a gallery with one or more side dolls. It is said to be balanced if the dolls are symmetrical about the central post. In 1962 these balanced SR four-aspect starting signals at **Holborn Viaduct** have electric route indicators (above) and shunting signals (below).

230 (*Below, left*): Looking from the Yatton direction, these home signals at **Wells** are mounted on a GWR wooden bracket. Photographed in 1962, the empty doll may once have carried an auxiliary signal. See *Plate 291* for the engine shed in detail.

231 (*Below, right*): For ease of observation from the Wolverhampton line, these home signals at **Stafford** were mounted more than 50ft high on an LNWR wooden bracket. The calling-on auxiliary signal is at low level. Photographed in 1962, the gap on the top gallery suggests that it may once have carried the auxiliary signal.

232 (*Above*): At **Stamford** (GNR) this LMS balanced bracket is for MR traffic from Stamford Town. For stability, the tall tubular steel dolls have guys and an intermediate tie bar. In 1963, LMS Class 4MT 2-6-4T No. 42103 heads a local train to Peterborough.

233 (*Right*): In 1962, this tubular steel left-hand bracket guards the joint GWR/LNWR station at **Condover**. The bracket is GWR in style but the conical finial is less common.

234 (*Below*): Going south, **Stafford Junction** is guarded by six stop signals with associated distant arms – up slow (left) and up fast (right). The raised arms are for the Wolverhampton line. The tall wooden balanced brackets are LNWR. In 1962, an LMS 'Jinty' 0-6-0T stands by the yard signal box (far right) while LMS 2-6-4 tank No. 42327 slips its wheels as it starts.

Stretched signalry

235 (*Above*): On the MR at **Stamford Town**, this wooden gantry with corner brackets is close to the overbridge, such that the home stop signal has been underslung. In 1963, LMS 8F class 2-8-0 No. 48752 hauls a brake van.

236 (*Below*): This GWR 'gallows' bracket at **Plymouth North Road** carries starting arms for the line beyond the platform. At rest on the near face in 1959, is GWR 'Castle' class 4-6-0 No. 5069 *Isambard Kingdom Brunel*.

237 (*Opposite, top*): The up gantry at **Tonbridge** bridged one track and was cantilevered over several others. Built by the SR in 1935, its latticework is as fine as lace, carrying an array of starting and auxiliary arms. Blowing off in 1960 is rebuilt SR light Pacific No. 34037 *Clovelly* with an up express.

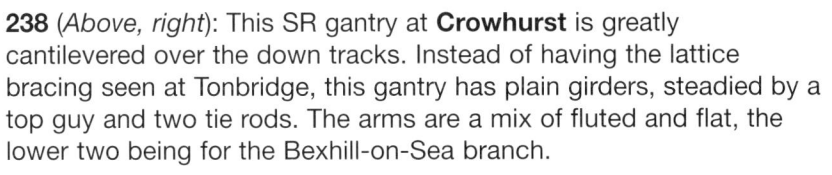

238 (*Above, right*): This SR gantry at **Crowhurst** is greatly cantilevered over the down tracks. Instead of having the lattice bracing seen at Tonbridge, this gantry has plain girders, steadied by a top guy and two tie rods. The arms are a mix of fluted and flat, the lower two being for the Bexhill-on-Sea branch.

239 (*Below*): The gantry at the west end of **Southampton Central** carried 13 semaphore arms. They guarded the down main (right), the down relief (centre) and the docks line (left). In 1959, ready to depart to Weymouth, is SR 'Lord Nelson' class 4-6-0 No. 30851 *Sir Francis Drake*.

Low platform boxes

Platforms were sometimes built around signal boxes of standard height with just a few steps to the operating room. Signalling Study Group classifications (*Ref. 1*) are used throughout the 14 pages which follow.

240 (*Above*): **Bookham,** between Leatherhead and Effingham Junction, had an LSWR Type 3a signal box, characterised by the upper lights and multiple window panes. Set back from the platform, it is brick to the operating floor with boards above. In 1963, the station boasted SR lamps, flower beds, encroaching trees and a large building.

241 (*Below*): On the NSR's Ashbourne branch, **Norbury** signal box could be 'in-house' or of McK&H origin. It has five wooden steps with a handrail. The gabled roof blends with the closed station building and house. In 1962, the tablet is exchanged with the pickup goods, headed by LMS 2-6-4 tank No. 42609. Note the old oil lamp, left.

242 In 1961, **Knockholt** had an SER vernacular signal box of brick and timber with an attached closet. The change of platform height suggests that it was once free-standing. Note the SER arc roof and valance of the platform shelter.

243 Rotherfield and Mark Cross had an LBSCR Type 1 box featuring a hipped roof and small decorative crosses in the top panels. The two steps to the operating room are in concrete. This 1959 scene is completed by a chair, fire buckets, a motorbike, flowers, signs and an SR rail-built signal assembly.

Timber signal boxes

Timber signal boxes were cheap to build but more expensive to maintain. Some were rarely, if ever repainted or repaired throughout the six or seven decades of their life.

244 Most SER signal boxes were timber in vernacular in-house style, as seen at **Sharnal Street**. Dating from the opening of the Hundred of Hoo line in 1882, the box became partially enclosed by an SR concrete platform when the down loop was reinstated in 1934. Photographed in 1959, the enamelled nameboard is BR.

245 This GNR Type 4a timber box at **Stamford** is piled into the bank of the River Welland. It is made distinctive by tall windows, decorative bargeboards and finials. Wooden props help to support the steps and closet. As well as serving the GNR terminus, it guarded the junction with the MR line from Stamford Town (right) with its lower-quadrant signals on a wooden post. The upper-quadrant signals (left) are LNER, mounted on tubular steel dolls on lattice brackets. Note the catch points and the foot-crossing to the box.

246 MR signal boxes were of in-house design. Neat characteristics included a hipped roof, conical finials, horizontal boarding to floor level, vertical boarding to window level and small window panes with 45° corners at the top. In 1963 on the Peterborough to Stamford line, **Uffington** displays its MR Type 3a, having tall windows at the front and sides. Note the empty yard and the lattice windows of the station building.

247 On the line southeast of Great Yarmouth, **St Olaves** had a GER Type 7 box. It looks mellow – all timber with large windows, central steps, large iron brackets, and a wooden nameboard on the gable end. In 1959, an additional duty of this signalman was to cycle to the New Cut to help lift the A143 drawbridge (see *Plate 160*). These days, the line to Yarmouth is closed and a new bridge carries the A143 over the canal.

Brick-to-floor boxes

The term 'brick-to-floor' means brick to the operating floor with timber above. Such signal boxes were commonly built until the 1930s when timber ceased to be used externally.

248 (*Right*): At **Stone Junction**, in 1962 this NSR Type 2 signal box has a steeply pitched gabled roof, a matching porch and windows three panes deep. The cleaning platform has a handrail but no guard rail. The signal post is LMS.

249 (*Below, right*): S&F Type 12a boxes are characterised by their generous roof overhang and deep windows. This one in 1961, on the SER at **Chilham**, has attractive steps, veranda and an entrance porch.

250 (*Below*): This LNWR Type 4 signal box has horizontal boarding above the operating floor, no overhang of the gable ends and little roof overhang at the sides. To fit the limited space between the tracks, **Nuneaton Up Sidings** had modest oversailing (jutting out on both sides). Note the ornate brickwork, the central drainpipe, a lamp and shunting loudspeaker (right). Like Stone Junction (*above*), there are no railings for window cleaning. Pictured in 1962, a few months before power signalling arrived, this box has great charm.

251 The North London line is quadruple until **Camden Road Junction** where it becomes double track for a few yards. In 1961, the junction was guarded by an NLR Type 3a box. The operating room has vertical boarding. Windows are cleaned by leaning out. The brick locking room is windowless. Steps rise above an extension for power signalling equipment. The right-hand line leads across murky suburbia via Hampstead Heath to Willesden Junction. The left-hand line leads directly to the LNWR main line via Primrose Hill.

252 Most LCDR signal boxes were supplied by Stevens or S&F. A few were built in-house, as seen at **Bat and Ball** on the outskirts of Sevenoaks. It has neat vertical boarding above the brick locking room (extended for power signalling). Like Bricklayers Arms and Elephant & Castle, the district was named after a pub.

Brick-to-roof boxes

253 Characteristics of the LSWR Type 4 box at **Worting Junction** are the hipped roof and central brick pillar at the front. Its original arc-headed windows have been replaced. In 1963, this three-car DEMU was probably on its way from Eastleigh Works for service on the GWR line between Basingstoke and Reading.

254 Duality in brick at the east end of **Faversham**: the old LCDR 'B' box, supplied by S&F, and the brand-new BR(S) box. A set of SR steam stock also contrasts with new EMUs waiting for 'E-Day' in the far sidings. In June 1959, SR 'Schools' class 4-4-0 No. 30921 *Shrewsbury* arrives with a train from Ramsgate.

255 The SR Type 14 signal box had ARP features (Air Raid Precautions) with brick sides, a concrete roof and some metal windows. On the SER main line in 1958, 4-SUB unit No. 4304 approaches **Petts Wood**. Originally a 3-SUB when built in 1925, it was augmented during the 1940s with a wider Bulleid coach (second here).

256 On the GWR/LNWR joint line between Shrewsbury and Welshpool, signal boxes were based upon S&F Type 1 but were wider and with decorative courses. This one at **Hanwood** had been extended. The signals and posts are of GWR design. In 1962, this was the junction for the Minsterley branch (left-hand track) which explains the facing point and multiple signals. Note the tablet-collecting apparatus by the level crossing, right.

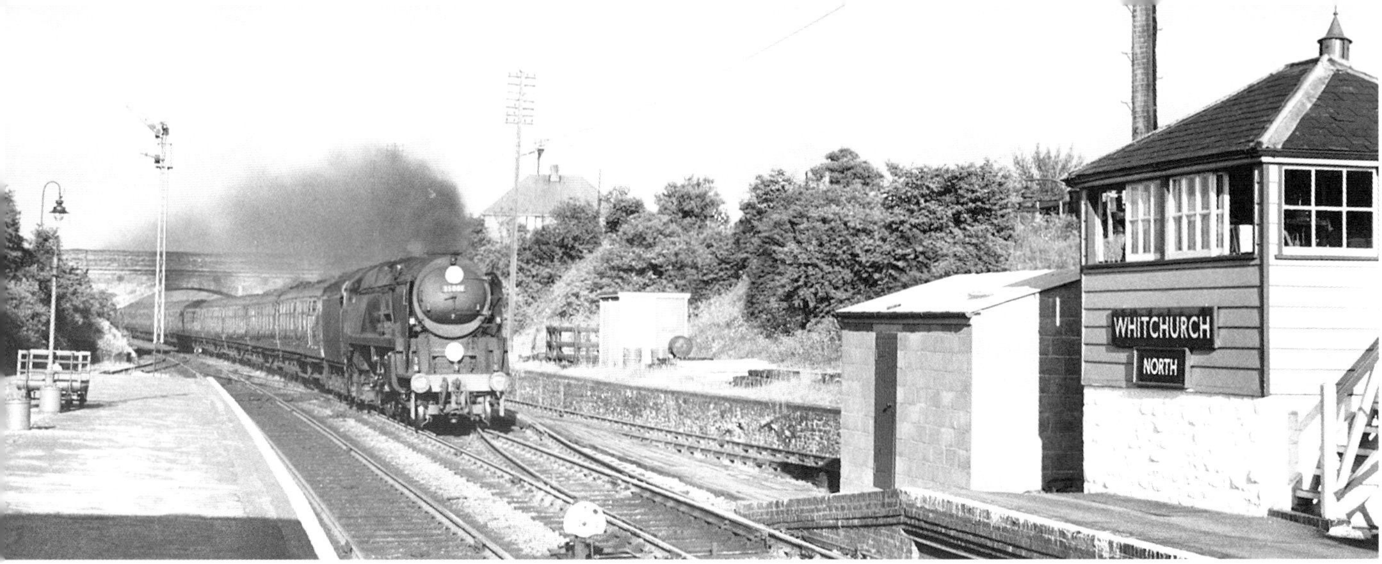
WHITCHURCH
NORTH

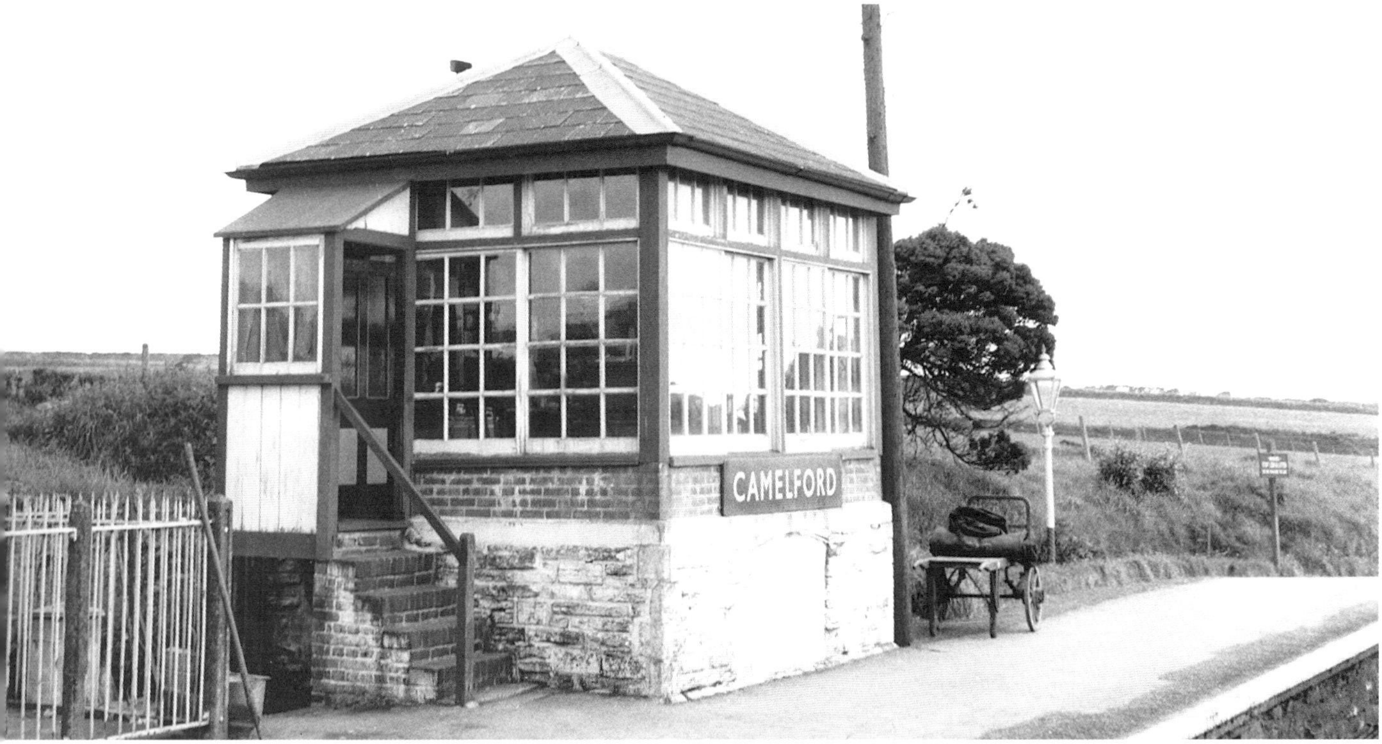
CAMELFORD

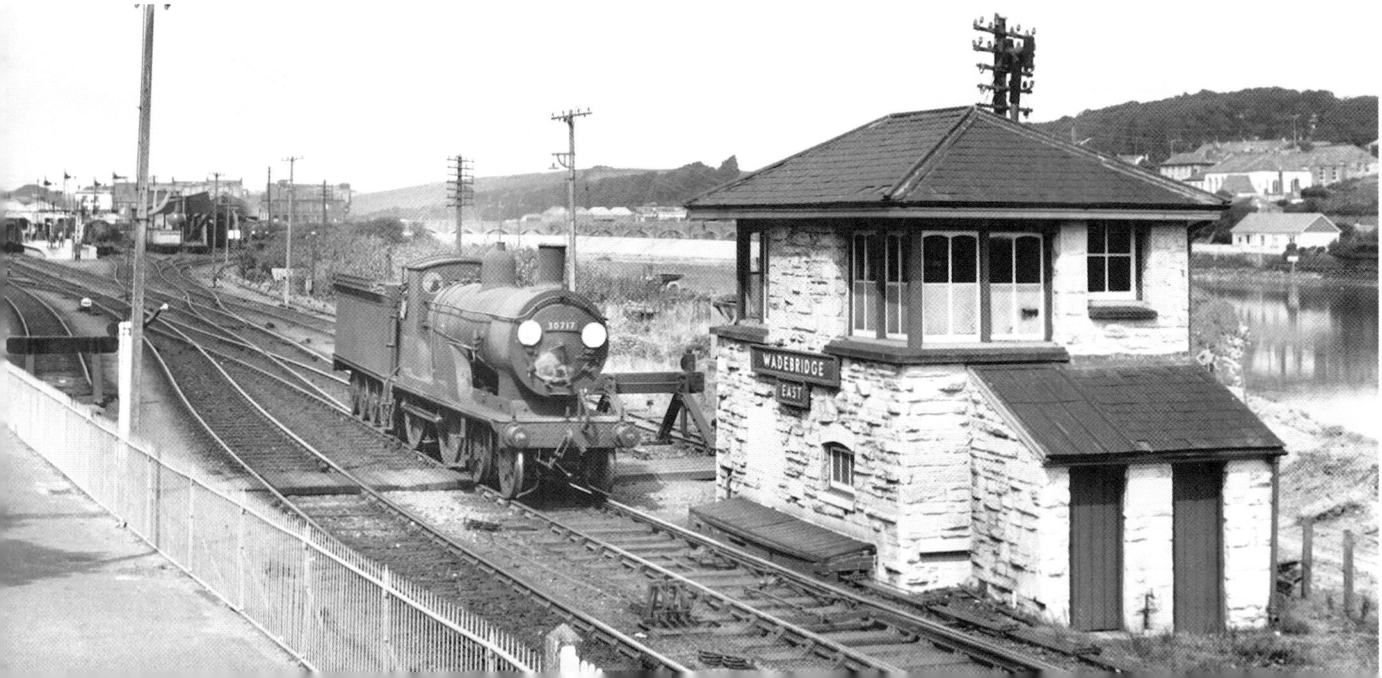
WADEBRIDGE
EAST

Stone and brick boxes

257 (*Opposite, top*): This LSWR stone-to-floor Type 1 platform box at **Whitchurch North** has lost its valance. In 1963, charging through with an express to Exeter, is SR 'Merchant Navy' Pacific No. 35001 *Channel Packet*, newly rebuilt.

258 (*Opposite, middle*): This LSWR Type 3c platform box at **Camelford** was originally stone-to-floor but the narrow timber section has been replaced with five courses of brick. Steps to the porch are also brick. In 1959, a shunter's pole rests on the railings. The barrow and gas lamp are LSWR.

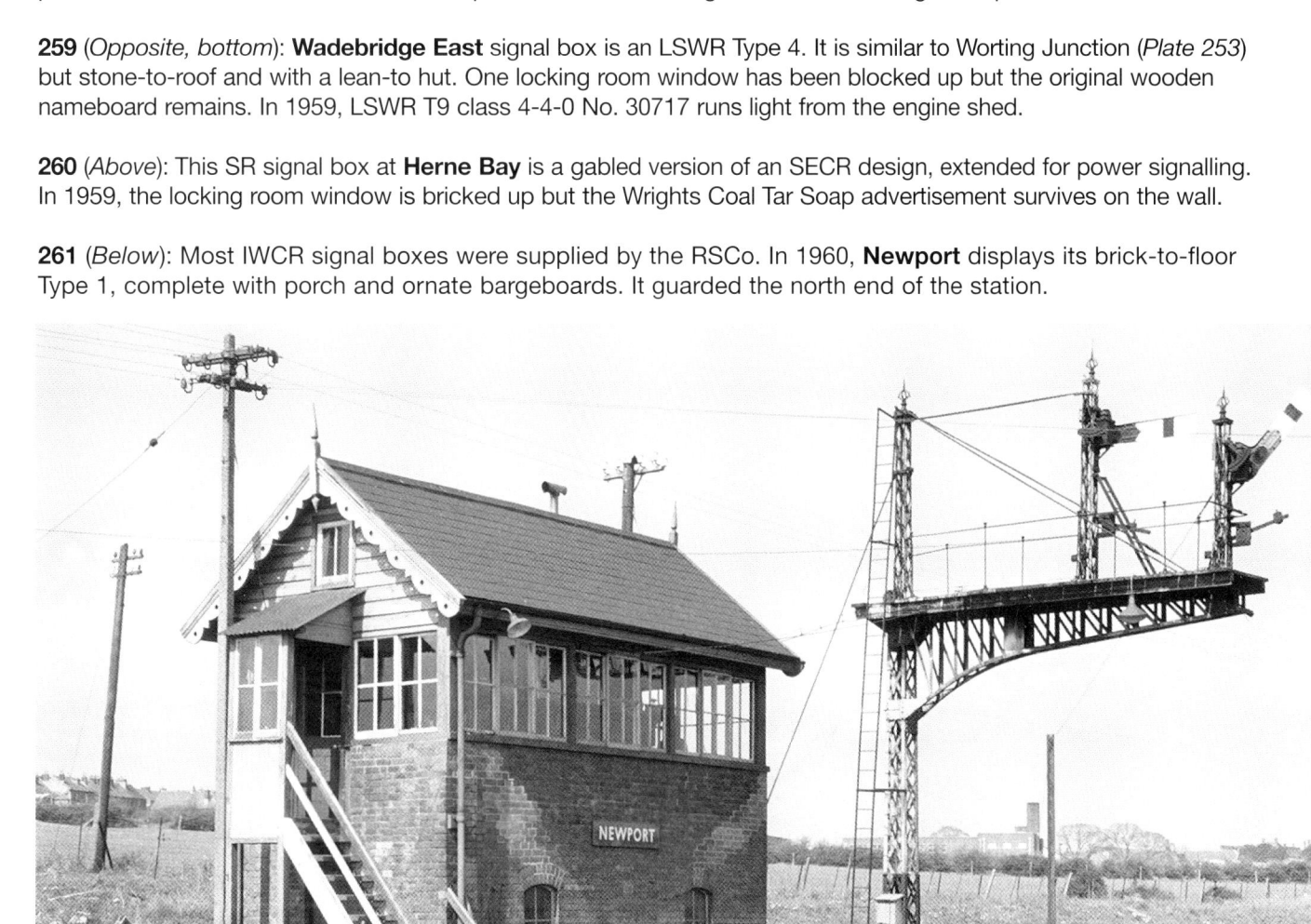

259 (*Opposite, bottom*): **Wadebridge East** signal box is an LSWR Type 4. It is similar to Worting Junction (*Plate 253*) but stone-to-roof and with a lean-to hut. One locking room window has been blocked up but the original wooden nameboard remains. In 1959, LSWR T9 class 4-4-0 No. 30717 runs light from the engine shed.

260 (*Above*): This SR signal box at **Herne Bay** is a gabled version of an SECR design, extended for power signalling. In 1959, the locking room window is bricked up but the Wrights Coal Tar Soap advertisement survives on the wall.

261 (*Below*): Most IWCR signal boxes were supplied by the RSCo. In 1960, **Newport** displays its brick-to-floor Type 1, complete with porch and ornate bargeboards. It guarded the north end of the station.

Signal box mechanisms

262 (*Below*): This LCDR signal box at **Canterbury East** has oversailing to either side. Unconventionally, it is supported on steel columns set in a concrete foundation, with all rods and wires entering the locking room from below. This creates a semi-protected open space, giving excellent access to the point rods and cranks, the signal-wires and wheels and some new terminal boxes. Pictured in 1959, one group of wheels (on an elevated inclined bar) leads to the right. A second group of pulleys, together with all the cranks, is at track level.

263 (*Opposite, top*): On the LBSCR secondary line between Dorking and Horsham, this low platform-box at **Holmwood** has a spacious tunnel built into the concrete platform – much easier for maintenance access than at Shanklin (*Plate 264*). The box is a brick example of an S&F Type 5, characterised by its hipped roof with generous overhang, round-cornered window tops and a row of top-lights, most of which were blanked off here in 1959. Note the fire buckets by the single step, also the wooden closet behind the privet hedge.

264 (*Below, left*): This S&F signal box at **Shanklin** was of similar height to Canterbury East but built into the up platform with covered steps on the right. By 1960, the locking room window had been blackened. The rods and wires exit through a wide but low tunnel built into the platform using lintels. The seats are LSWR (centre) and 'Best Kept Station' (left, won by Shanklin in 1959.) The posters advertise car ferries and some obscure product called Spree.

265 (*Below, right*): In Spring 1962 on the Wolverhampton line south of Stafford, **Penkridge** still had a goods yard and a signal box. The LNWR lever frame is characterised by loop-handles for the catch rods and a separate rear-board for the lever nameplates. Note the oil lamp and the age-distorted glass.

Signal box variations

266 (*Right*): South of Oxted, a number of LBSCR stations had a lever frame on the platform by the booking office, protected by railings and the canopy. By 1963, this one at **Cowden** had been bricked in, with windows above.

267 (*Below, left*): Southwest of Peterborough, **Barnwell** had an LNWR outside ground frame set into the platform with no railings or canopy. Photographed in 1963, *Plate 188* shows a second outside frame at this station.

268 (*Below, right*): An outside ground frame in 1961 on the SER's Westerham branch at **Brasted**. Lever functions were: plunger release, point operation and spare. The frame is mounted crudely on timbers. (See *Plate 82* for the associated pointwork.)

269 (*Opposite*): Reproduced here to about full size, a double-sided GWR notice regarding signalling alterations at **Bramley** (south of Reading). Issued in 1939, it was rescued from the signal box in 1963.

Signal Box

PRIVATE and not for Publication.　　　　　　NOTICE No. E.58.

GREAT WESTERN RAILWAY.

(For the use of the Company's Servants only.)

Notice to Enginemen, Guards, etc.

TUESDAY, NOVEMBER 28th, 1939.

SIGNAL ALTERATIONS—
BRAMLEY SIGNAL BOX

Between the hours of 7.30 a.m. and 4.30 p.m. the Signal Engineers will be engaged in bringing into use a Single Disc at the points leading from the dead end Siding to Sidings Nos. 2 and 3, and a Double Disc at the points leading from Sidings Nos. 2 and 3 to the dead end Siding.

A new connection will be brought into use as shewn on the diagram appended.

During the time the work is being carried out Bramley Up and Down Distant Signals will be disconnected and placed at "Caution."

All arrangements for the safe working of the Line (including the appointment of Hand Signalmen) must be made by the District Inspector in accordance with Rule 77.

Paddington Station,　　　　　　　　　　C. T. COX,
　November 15th, 1939.　　　　　　　　Divisional Superintendent.

The receipt of this Notice to be acknowledged by first Train.

1,000—11-39.　2658.

- -

..................Department..................Station................1939.
　Received copy of Notice No. E.58, dated November 15th, in connection with Signal Alterations, Bramley.

C. T. COX, Esq.,　　　　　..................(Signature).
　PADDINGTON.

Re-used coaches

270 (*Above*): An SECR first/second composite, built around 1900. Becoming all-third in 1929, it was withdrawn in 1943 to become an engineers' mess room, No. DS1838 (*Ref. 7*). Photographed at **Hildenborough** in 1960.

271 (*Right*): An SECR 'birdcage' brake-third, built during 1912-15. Withdrawn in 1956, it was then used for Civil Defence Training (*Ref. 8*) as No. DS132. Photographed at **East Croydon** in 1963.

272 (*Below*): Two LSWR lavatory brake-thirds re-used from the late 1940s as a breakdown train unit. Photographed at **Fratton** in 1958.

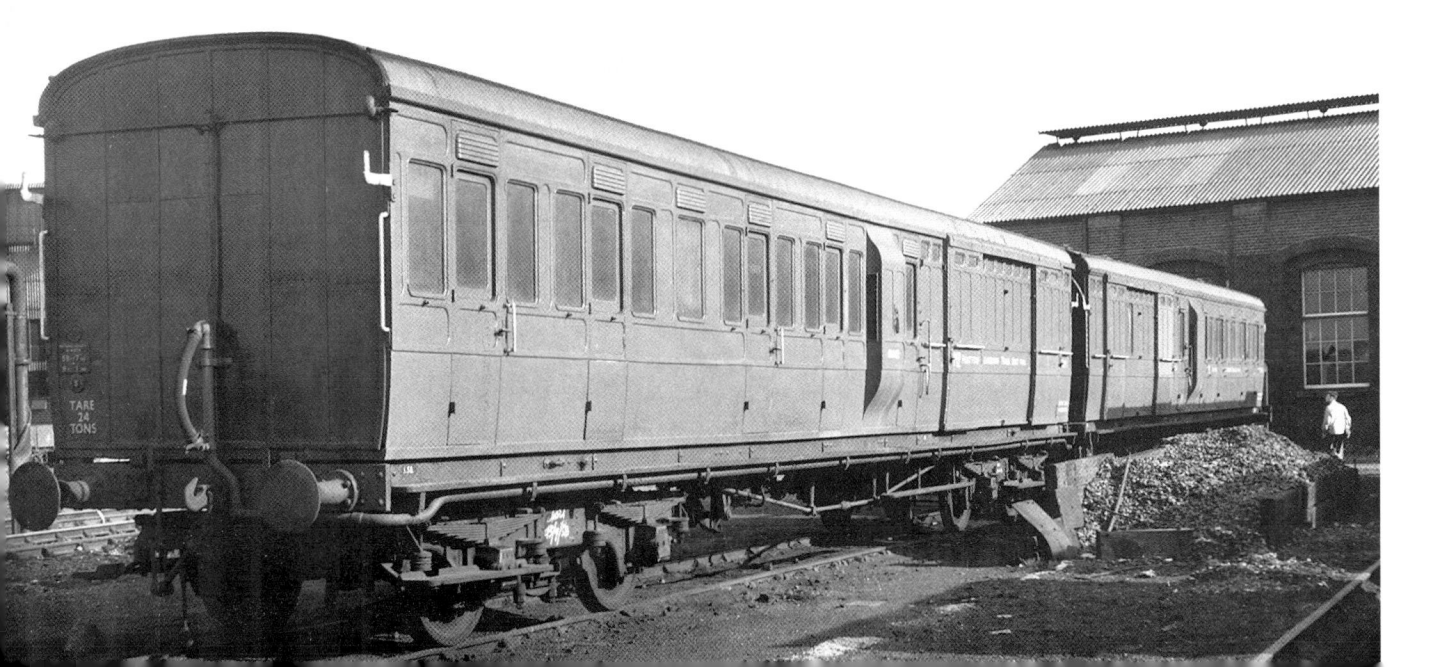

273 (*Above*): A Pullman car re-used as a camping coach at **Corfe Castle** (LSWR). Making smoke in 1963 is SR Q class 0-6-0 No. 30535 with a branch train from Swanage. This station today is preserved for steam and diesel operation by the Swanage Railway.

274 (*Left*): An SECR coach reused for staff accommodation at **Chichester**. It is isolated in a bay platform by a rail-built buffer stop in 1958.

275 (*Below*): An unlikely group of coaches on a **Stafford** siding in 1962: on the right, two BR sleeping cars; on the left, part of an EMU built by Siemens in 1914 for the LNWR shuttle service over the West London line between Willesden Junction and Earls Court. In 1951, such stock was transferred to the MR's Lancaster to Heysham branch for BR electrification trials at 50Hz. This coach looks like a motor brake third with the pantograph and electrical equipment removed to make an additional passenger compartment at the far end. Awaiting stringing, the OHE gantries are already blackened from steam exhaust.

Passenger brakes

276 SR passenger vans were developed from SECR designs, having distinctive wooden panelling of two thick and two narrow bands alternately. There were four-wheel and bogie variations, both with and without a brake compartment. This 36ft four-wheel passenger brake was in service at **Sandwich** in 1964.

277 LNER passenger vans from the Gresley era had distinctive teak panelling and domed roof ends. This variation, a 61ft 6in vestibuled brake, was photographed at **Peterborough East** in 1963. The wooden signal posts are GER, possibly the barrows too. The straight-fluted lamp standards might be GER or even ECR.

278 In 1958, 4-SUB unit No. 4505 stops on the Brighton side of **Peckham Rye**. It is a mid-1920s conversion of LBSCR wooden steam stock from around 1910. This motor coach has an all-steel SR motorman's cab with a large compartment behind for luggage and the guard, including a small lookout ducket.

279 A train of post-war GWR steel-clad non-corridor stock pauses at **Llanfyllin** in 1962. The unfolding story is: the train has shortly arrived; passengers are departing; luggage awaits loading from the barrow; the guard is opening the luggage compartment doors, and some new passengers have already boarded.

Lonesome wagons

280 (*Right*): In 1962, a branch goods train departs **Llanfyllin** towards the CR main line at Llanymynech. Headed by Ivatt Mogul No. 46519, it comprises one goods van and a GWR brake van.

281 (*Below*): In 1962, four varieties of covered van stand in a siding at **Welshpool**. The station is CR but with a GWR covered footbridge and signals. The huge canopy looks like an add-on with its multiple posts.

282 (*Opposite, top*): In 1960 on the MNR, two open wagons stand in a grassy siding at **Ballaugh**. Blowing off is 2-4-0 tank No. 8 *Fenella* with a train from Ramsey to Douglas.

283 (*Opposite, middle*): In 1961, all that remained of the former East Kent Railway was a few miles of track from Shepherds Well to **Tilmanstone Colliery.** Presumably, an accident had upturned this GCR five-plank wagon.

284 (*Opposite, bottom*): Condemned wooden wagons were stored on the northern section of the Bluebell line in 1959 and this assortment is at **Kingscote**. Note the LBSCR canopies and the wartime striping on the posts.

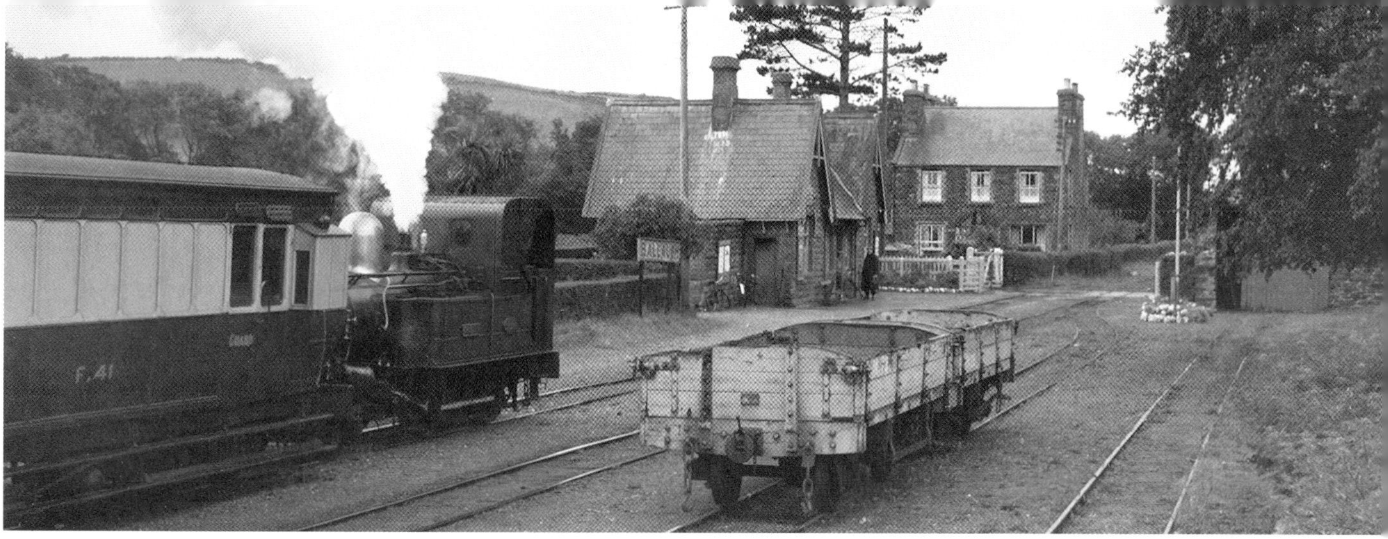
F.41

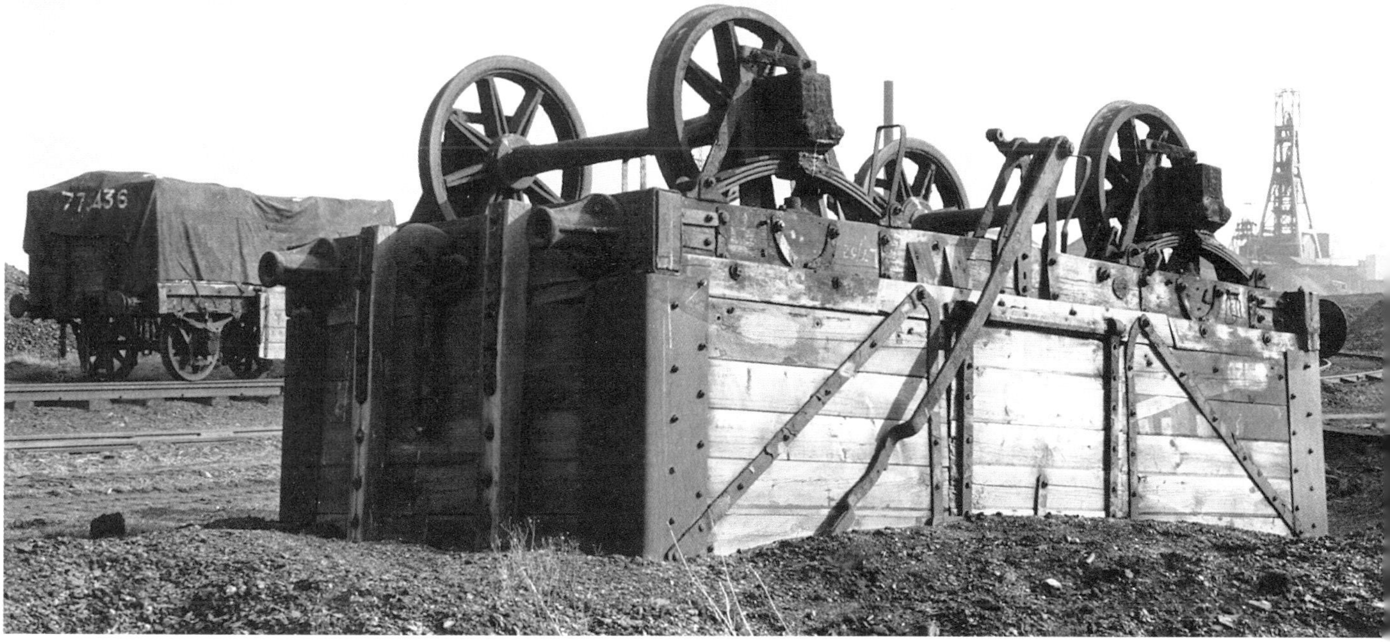
77436

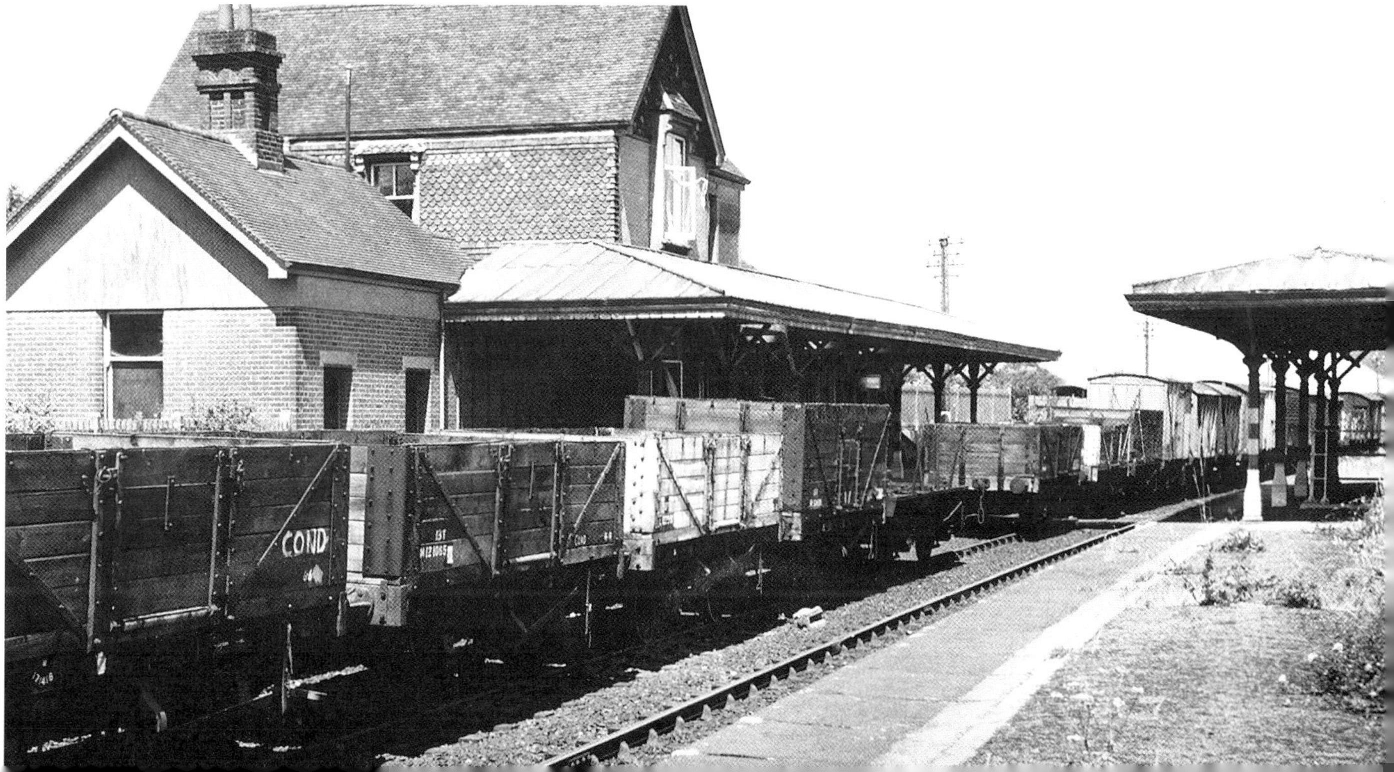
COND

Grounded bodies

285 (*Right*): In 1960, this four-wheel passenger brake body adorned the works yard at **Newport**. Its origin is not known. The windows, door handles, guard's ducket and roof profile resemble those of some MR 12-wheel composites bought by the IWCR in 1909. The hand rails, however, are quite different.

286 (*Below*): In 1962, just south of Shrewsbury, the rotting remains of **Meole Brace Halt** are partially sheltered by the A5 road bridge. A wagon body has been added to the wooden platform and shelter. The S&MR ran parallel here with the GWR/LNWR joint line and was intended originally, to be extended to the Potteries.

287 (*Opposite, top*): In 1963 at **Barnwell** on the LNWR's Nene Valley line, a van body was in use for platform storage. The small wooden station building has vernacular charm, its plainness relieved by the canopy whose brackets and valance are elaborate. The brick station bungalow beyond is more substantial (see also *Plate 23*). The station nameboard is nicely painted. The metal structure (left) was originally the Gent's urinal.

288 Seen in 1962, two compartments of an old coach end their days surrounded by debris in a goods yard at **Stafford**. The roof profile, panelling and round-cornered windows indicate MR origin.

289 Most rolling stock on the Isle of Wight was second-hand from the mainland. These Metropolitan Railway bodies ended their lives on **St Helens** sea front as beach huts (one per compartment), and seen here in 1960. They were rigid eight-wheelers. The doors were round-topped in case of opening in tunnels. See *Plate 213* for a 4-4-0 tank engine which might have hauled such a train through London's tunnels.

Small MPDs

290 In 1963, sand and ash litter the closed **Stamford MPD** but the coaling stage and GNR shed are empty and crane-less. Note the oil lamp, the great water tank and the tall balanced signal bracket.

291 At the GWR's compact depot at **Wells**, the coaling platform and jib crane were located beneath the water tank. This was supported on an elaborate iron structure of tubular columns, brackets and rectangular frame. The two roads have ash pits, a water column and a gas lamp. There are further gas lamps on the far side by the coal siding. In 1962, BR Standard Class 3MT 2-6-2T No. 82007 stands in the two-road brick shed.

292 Peel shed nestled between mountains and the main line level-crossing. Facilities comprised a single-track wooden shed, a small wooden office, a steel water tank set upon a massive stone base, and manual point levers with a 180° throw. In 1960, 2-4-0 tank No. 5 *Mona* is beautifully clean. Note the oil cans on the buffer beam and the screw jack on the side tank. Sadly, the line to Peel closed in 1968, becoming a footpath.

293 In 1960, IMR 2-4-0 tank No. 16 *Mannin* poses outside **Port Erin**'s single-road engine shed. Built of stone, the shed has apparently been extended. Note the great water tank, the small piles of ash and the simplest of point levers. The hoarding advertises Bill Duncan on the organ and Ivy Benson with her all-lady orchestra – both are in summer season at Douglas.

Large MPDs

294 (*Above*): On shed in 1962 at **Craven Arms** are LMS 8F class 2-8-0 No. 48732 and GWR 0-6-0 No. 3205.

295 (*Below*): An SR light Pacific and two BR Standards are on shed in 1963 at **Bournemouth**. In charge of the trains are LSWR M7 class 0-4-4 tanks Nos 30052 and 30127. The hoist tower served a maintenance siding.

296 (*Opposite, top*): On shed in 1959 at **Dover** are a rebuilt SR light Pacific (left), SER O1 class 0-6-0 No. 31425 (of 1897 vintage) and SR 'Merchant Navy' heavy Pacific No. 35028 *Clan Line* arriving with a boat train. The old SR shed looks run-down.

297 (*Opposite, middle*): Seen at **Stewarts Lane** in 1960 are LBSCR 0-6-0 C2X class No. 32438, SECR H class 0-4-4T No. 31550 and a BR Standard 2-6-4T. Note the coal and ash sidings and water columns.

298 (*Opposite, bottom*): On shed at **Nuneaton** in 1962 are a diesel shunter and a mix of LMS and BR Standard locomotives. The telegraph pole holds seven spars and has a bracing prop at one side. Other poles are for yard lamps, signal-wires, OHE gantries (under construction), and an LNWR signal bracket.

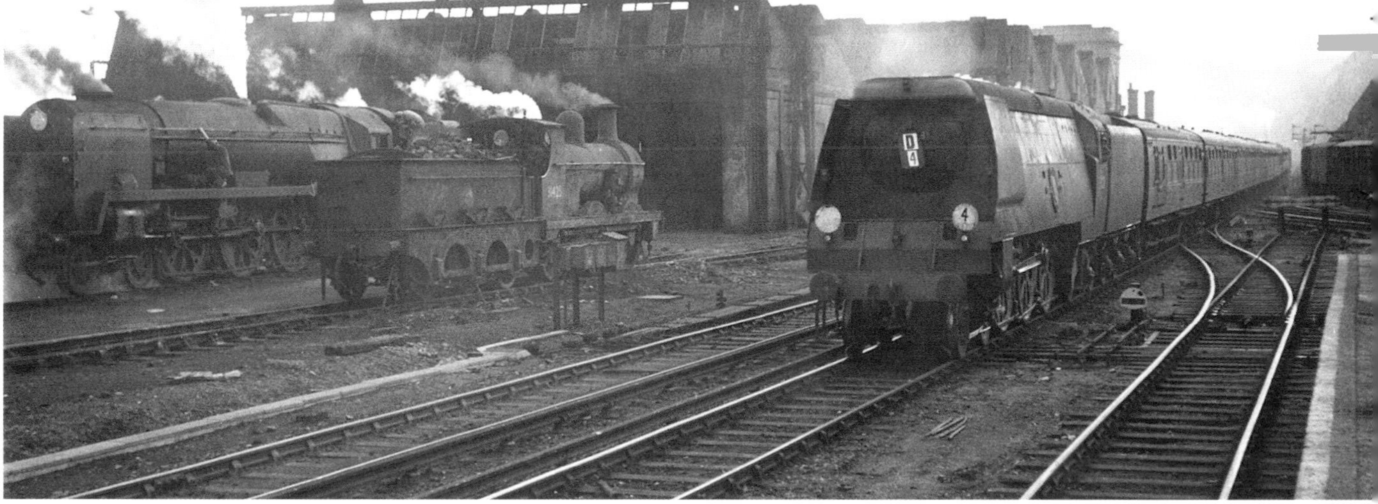
D4
4

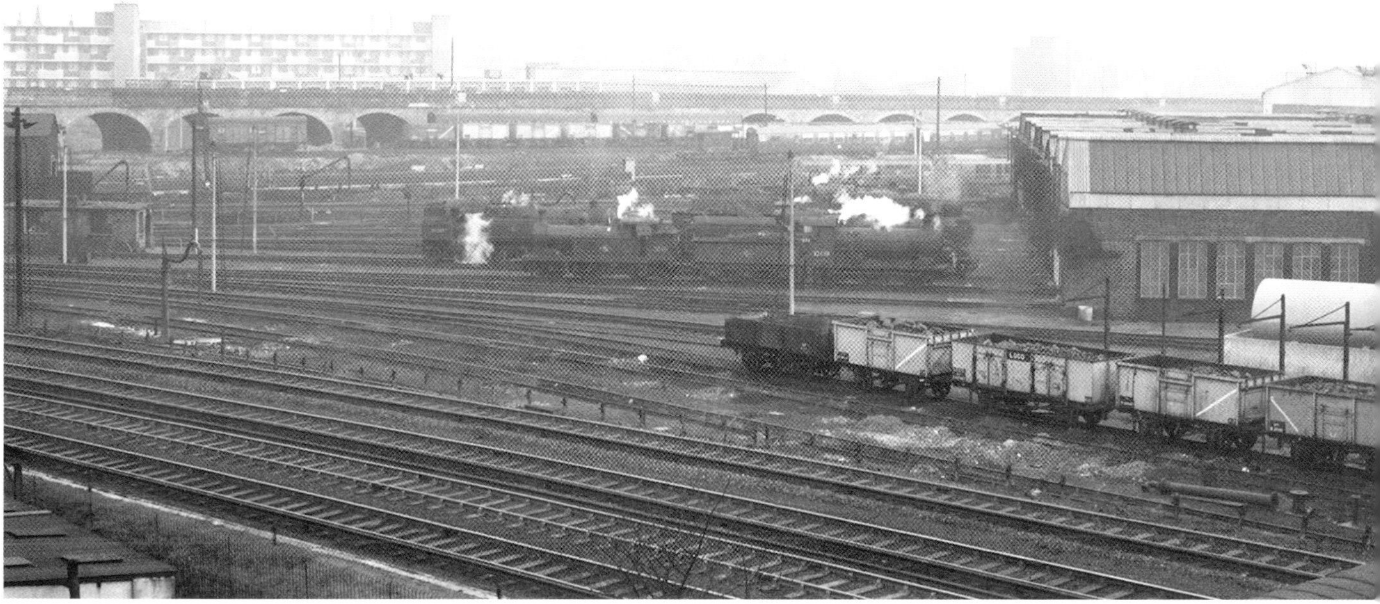

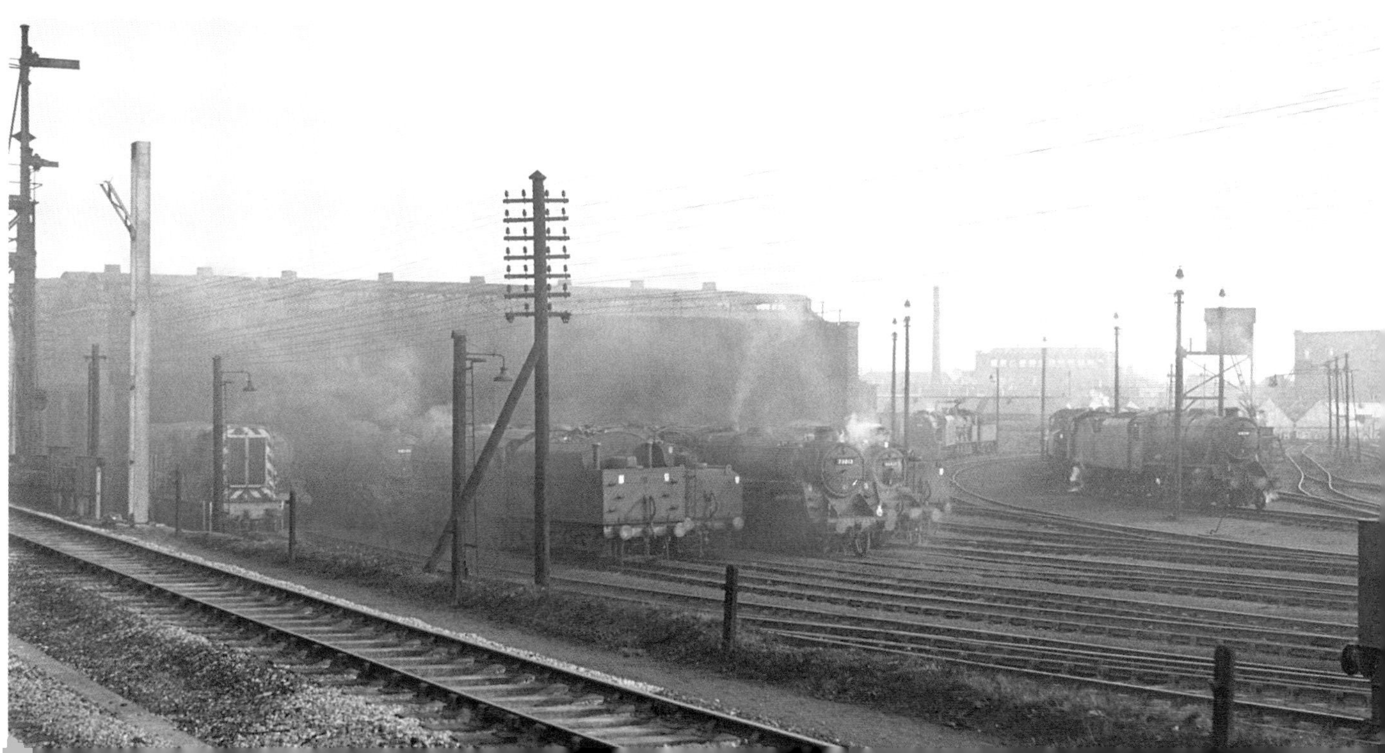

Steam servicing

299 (*Right*): At the S&DJR MPD at **Templecombe**, the ashing pit has an electric yard lamp and a selection of shovels and rakes (alas with few on the rack). In 1963, wooden wagons were stored here, ready for scrapping. The locomotive is GWR 2251 class 0-6-0 No. 3216.

300 (*Below*): On shed at **Stafford** in 1962 are BR Standard 4-6-0 No. 73025 and LMS 2-6-4T No. 42546 (taking water by the ferro-concrete 'cenotaph' coaling tower). Note the wooden platelayers' hut (with brick chimney), a tall LMS yard lamp, brick offices, the six-road LMS engine shed (of steel and brick), a new OHE gantry, new colour-light signals and the simple point levers with guard rails.

301 Two GWR Collett 0-6-0s and Ivatt Class 2MT 2-6-2T No. 41296 are on shed at **Templecombe** in 1963. Services include the turntable, water columns, coaling docks and assorted offices on the left.

302 The terminus at **Liverpool Central** was owned by the Cheshire Lines Committee until Nationalisation in 1948. This corner for locomotive servicing was compact and enclosed by stone walls. Reversing on to the turntable in 1960 is LMS Class 5MT 4-6-0 No. 45333. A water column, a pile of ash and half a dozen electric lamps complete the scene.

Water columns

303 When adjacent to the track, the simplest type of water column comprised a valve, a standpipe, a top bend and a flexible hose. This seaside example is at **Padstow**, the westernmost terminus of the LSWR. Engines would turn here, sometimes returning to Wadebridge for overnight stabling and coaling. In 1959, Bulleid SR light Pacific No. 34058 *Sir Frederick Pile* will turn, take water and probably drop ash.

304 This 1932 water column at **Allhallows-on-Sea** was integral with the circular water tank and served both platforms. Mounted on a girder pedestal, it is a type more commonly found on the GWR. Photographed in 1960, the signal bracket and loading gauge are SR. See *Plate 81* for the station layout.

305 Taking water at **Douglas** in 1960, a hose feeds through the cab side to the side tank. On shed (left to right) are Beyer Peacock 2-4-0 tanks No. 16 *Mannin*, No. 6 *Peveril*, No. 11 *Maitland*, No. 13 *Kissack* and No. 10 *G. H. Wood*. The shed and IMR works stand beyond. The coal was loaded manually here using baskets.

306 This self-centring type of water column at **Blandford Forum** was commonly found on the LSWR. In 1963, BR Standard Class 5MT 4-6-0 No. 73047 slips its wheels as it restarts a train of Bulleid stock up the S&DJR towards Bath. Shunting in the siding is GWR 0-6-0 pannier tank No. 4691.

Water towers

307 (*Above*): On the MR at **Derby**, a tall timber trestle supports a massive water tank. In 1960, Johnson 3-cylinder 4-4-0 compound No. 1000 is seen in MR livery. Built at Derby in 1902, it was withdrawn in 1951 for use on 'steam specials' and is now in the NRM, York. It is coupled here to diesel-electric shunter No. D3988.

308 (*Below, left*): On the LSWR at **Southampton Central**, cross-braced steel girders support a water tank with a pitched roof. In 1963, BR Standard Class 4MT Mogul No. 76028 heads an up freight train.

309 (*Below*): On the S&DJR at **Sturminster Newton**, a solid stone plinth supports a modest water tank with an integral hose. It looks as if the tank height has been increased with three extra courses of brick. Photographed in 1963, the Bournemouth platform has an intriguing dip for the staff crossing.

310 (*Above, left*): On the CR at **Llanfyllin**, tubular steel columns support a water tank with integral hose. The signals and bracket are GWR. In 1962, Ivatt Mogul No. 46509 departs with the branch train, to Llanymynech.

311 (*Above, right*): On the LCDR at **Ashford West**, this massive water tank is supported on a tall brick building, big enough to house a water pump or other equipment. A service trolley stands in front, in 1958.

312 (*Below*): On the LSWR at **Axminster**, a brick pump house supports a large water tank with an arc roof. The water pump is driven by a steam engine which exhausts into the brick chimney. Photographed in 1959 with LSWR 'Radial' tank No. 30583 taking coal in the Lyme Regis branch bay.

Abbreviations

BRC&W	Birmingham Railway Carriage & Wagon Co.
BR	British Railways (1948 on)
BTC	British Transport Commission
DEMU	Diesel-electric multiple unit
DMU	Diesel multiple unit
EMU	Electric multiple unit
EPB	EMU with electro-pneumatic brakes
LM	London Midland (BR Region)
LT	London Transport
McK&H	McKenzie & Holland (signalling company)
MPD	Motive Power Depot
MT	Mixed Traffic
OHE	Overhead electrification
RCTS	Railway Correspondence & Travel Society
RSCo	Railway Signalling Company
S&F	Saxby & Farmer (signalling company)
SSG	Signalling Study Group (Ref. 1)
2-BIL	Two-car EMU with lavatories
4-COR	Four-car express EMU with corridors
4-SUB	Four-car suburban EMU

Grouped railways (1923-47)

GWR	Great Western Railway
LMS	London, Midland & Scottish Railway
LNER	London & North Eastern Railway
SR	Southern Railway

Pre-Grouping (pre-1923) and independent railways

C&WR	Canterbury & Whitstable Railway
CR	* Cambrian Railways
ECR	** Eastern Counties Railway
EKR	East Kent Railway
GCR	Great Central Railway
GER	Great Eastern Railway
GNR	Great Northern Railway
GWR	Great Western Railway
HR	Highland Railway
IMR	Isle of Man Railway
IWCR	Isle of Wight Central Railway
IWR	Isle of Wight Railway
LBSCR	London, Brighton & South Coast Railway
LCDR	London, Chatham & Dover Railway
LNWR	London & North Western Railway
LSWR	London & South Western Railway
Met.	Metropolitan Railway
MNR †	Manx Northern Railway
MR	Midland Railway
NLR	North London Railway
NSR	North Staffordshire Railway
PD&SWJR	Plymouth, Devonport & South Western Junction Railway
S&DJR	+ Somerset & Dorset Joint Railway
S&MR	Shropshire & Montgomeryshire Railway
SECR	++ South Eastern & Chatham Railway
SER	South Eastern Railway

*	The GWR absorbed the CR in 1922.
**	The ECR became part of the GER in 1862.
+	Jointly owned by the LSWR and MR.
++	A merger in 1899 of the LCDR and SER.
†	The IMR absorbed the MNR in 1905.

References

1. Signalling Study Group, *The Signal Box, a Pictorial History*, OPC, 1986.
2. Postlethwaite, Alan, *Odd Corners of the Southern from the Days of Steam*, Sutton Publishing, 1998.
3. Postlethwaite, Alan, *More Odd Corners of the Southern from the Days of Steam*, Sutton Publishing, 2001.
4. Postlethwaite, Alan, *Adventurous Model Railway Plans*, PSL-Haynes Publishing, 2003.
5. Buck, Gordon, *A Pictorial Survey of Railway Stations*, OPC, 1992.
6. *Railway Magazine* March 1961 *Metropolitan Tank Engine Restored*.
7. Kidner, R. W., *Service Stock of the Southern Railway*, Oakwood Press, 1993.
8. Gould, David, *Bogie Carriages of the SECR*, Oakwood Press, 1993.

Index

Lineside features
Ballast bins 105, 219, 273
Bridges, brick 37, 51, 149, 165, 166, 167, 178, 196, 222, 226, 227, 235
Bridges, steel 28, 30, 33, 44, 56, 76, 109, 120, 127, 157, 159-164, 168, 179, 196, 228, 286, 308
Bridges, stone 34, 72, 142, 156, 257
Cuttings 1, 51, 83, 94, 98, 115, 120, 130, 140, 141, 142, 149, 169, 170, 173-176, 199, 202, 226, 242, 280
Embankments 116, 118, 132, 137, 139, 146, 177-180
Fences 6, 7, 9, 22, 53, 59, 60, 67, 75, 79, 88, 92, 94, 116, 129, 132, 134, 165, 167, 177, 200, 202, 225, 231, 241
Gradient/mile posts 82, 142, 166, 174, 176, 273
Grindstones 140, 203
Huts 19, 20, 32, 73, 92, 94, 105, 126, 140, 170, 172, 173, 198, 200-204, 218, 220, 223, 227, 253, 257, 259, 287, 291, 292, 300, 301, 310
Industries 8, 153-156, 175, 283, 294
Rivers and sea 139, 157-160, 245, 259, 289, 303
Signs, cast-iron 6, 101, 181-187, 214, 215
Tunnels 154, 166, 169, 170-174, 226
Urban backdrops 30, 68, 69, 84, 96, 105, 148-152, 154, 197, 213, 226, 235, 251
Walls 14, 59, 150, 154, 171, 302
Wild flowers 72, 78, 98, 120, 169, 177, 179, 204, 222, 280, 310

Locomotive facilities
Ashing 248, 290, 291, 293, 299, 302, 303
Coaling 290, 291, 295, 300, 305
Sheds, large 272, 294-298, 300
Sheds, single-road 70, 290, 292, 293
Sheds, two-road 230, 291, 301, 305
Turntables 81, 301, 302, 303
Water columns 41, 57, 108, 128, 235, 248, 272, 291, 292, 297, 301-306, 309, 310
Water tanks/towers 41, 70, 281, 290, 291, 292, 304, 307-312
Works 3, 147, 305

Locomotives and train types
0-6-0   58, 105, 109, 118, 120, 139, 273, 294, 296, 297, 299, 301
2-6-0   47, 116, 121, 122, 127, 160, 224, 280, 308, 310
2-8-0   13, 235, 294, 313
2-10-0   220, 222
4-4-0   41, 98, 254, 259, 307
4-6-0   1, 23, 50, 94, 115, 126, 131, 144, 145, 188, 198, 202, 203, 204, 236, 239, 295, 298, 300, 302, 306, 313
4-6-2   4, 26, 96, 123, 151, 152, 169, 179, 197, 237, 257, 295, 296, 303
0-4-2T   48, 49, 95
0-4-4T   29, 55, 73, 114, 147, 149, 166, 178, 200, 295, 297
0-6-0T   33, 136, 137, 153, 205, 209, 234, 306
0-6-2T   2, 162, 291
2-4-0T   70, 133, 146, 180, 282, 292, 293, 305
2-6-2T   44, 57, 93, 95, 119, 129, 135, 138, 173, 176, 177, 301
2-6-4T   35, 130, 134, 168, 175, 193, 232, 234, 241, 297, 300
4-4-0T   213
4-4-2T   312
Coal/mineral trains 13, 115, 116, 118
Condensing engines 162, 213
Diesel 59, 99, 100, 108, 140-143, 165, 228

Diesel shunters 102, 158, 298, 307
DEMU 27, 91, 253
DMU 37, 42, 61, 76, 90, 91, 128, 198, 215, 225
EMU 28, 31, 45, 46, 56, 69, 132, 161, 163, 212, 255, 278
General freight trains 39, 105, 108, 109, 119-123, 134, 158, 193, 202, 241, 280
Mixed passenger-freight trains 129, 180, 199
Parcels trains 1, 18, 94-98
Push-pull trains 48, 49, 55, 73, 135, 137, 166, 200, 295
Steam specials 2, 162

Platform features
Barrows 2, 22, 24, 26, 34, 39, 42, 60, 85, 90-93, 101, 143, 198, 257, 258, 260, 274, 277, 279
Bays 55, 68, 274
Clocks 16, 19, 22
Coal bins 251, 272
Concrete platforms 2, 18, 21, 40, 46, 47, 51, 56, 68, 86, 143, 197, 239, 242, 244, 260, 263, 304, 308
Fire buckets 4, 243, 252, 263
Flag stones 48, 53, 57, 59, 65, 74, 93, 95, 100, 101
Flowers 20, 22, 24, 30, 39, 45, 50, 58-61, 75, 99
Footbridges, covered, 35, 46, 48, 281
Footbridges, enclosed 45, 47, 198
Footbridges, open, concrete 8, 43
Footbridges, open, lattice 1, 41, 42, 68, 85, 307
Footbridges, open, plated 44, 308
Grass 49, 52, 76, 86, 87, 104, 284
Island/peninsular platforms 27, 30, 32, 33, 69, 81, 91, 143
Lamps, electric 2, 27, 31, 32, 37, 42, 45, 51, 53, 56, 58, 59, 67, 68, 79, 99, 198, 240, 242, 277
Lamps, gas 7, 30, 43, 50, 54, 55, 57, 69, 197
Lamps, oil 14, 20, 24, 39, 40, 76, 77, 79, 241, 256, 258
Parcels/mail/luggage 15, 18, 42, 90, 91, 95, 110, 279
Passengers 2, 15, 18, 25-28, 30, 37, 42, 46, 48, 50, 55, 100, 135, 143, 198, 239, 279
Platforms, stone 42, 71, 72
Platforms, wooden 6, 31, 32, 75, 77, 78, 79, 161, 286
Posters 4, 12, 13, 19, 24, 34, 38, 48, 53, 64, 110, 154, 264
Railings 7, 40, 43, 51, 58, 74, 76, 77, 130, 258, 259
Railwaymen 5, 9, 26, 41, 90, 95, 101, 102, 143, 144, 147, 162, 168, 239, 241, 247, 260, 279, 302, 307, 308
Seats/benches 4, 20, 24, 27, 45, 58, 59, 60, 74, 76, 85, 92, 95, 99, 264, 312
Shelters 4, 18, 22, 24, 43, 37, 49-53, 60, 76-79, 85, 99, 102, 287
Signs, concrete/tiled 16, 68
Signs, enamelled 9, 12, 13, 16, 24, 27, 31, 53, 55, 62, 65, 66, 67, 74, 79, 102, 103, 133, 163, 194, 197, 223, 242, 243, 244, 249, 251, 252, 257, 258, 260, 261
Signs, wooden 4, 34, 39, 49, 75, 77, 78, 93, 241, 263, 287

Road transport
Bikes/motorbikes 5, 9, 18, 38, 243, 247
Buses/caravans 81, 209, 304
Cars 5, 8, 10, 12, 15, 80, 117, 154, 273
Vans/lorries 5, 11, 15, 42, 110, 213

Rolling stock
Bogie wagons 104, 210
Flat trucks 33, 57, 93, 128, 154, 228
Cattle wagons/horse boxes 34, 104, 129
Covered vans 50, 58, 96, 97, 106, 112, 193, 280, 281, 308
Goods brakes 104, 105, 234, 235, 280, 306
Grounded bodies 87, 117, 285-289
Hopper wagons 88, 193
Open trucks, steel 57, 104, 106, 109, 116, 118, 153, 297

Open trucks, wooden 39, 113, 116, 118, 282, 283, 284, 299
Parcels vans 1, 94-98, 151, 204, 276, 277, 295
Passenger brakes 276-279
Re-used coaches 270-275, 278
Sleeping cars 275
Tank wagons 89, 129

Signal boxes
Brick 74, 106, 108, 253-256, 263, 266,
Brick with timber 20, 56, 92, 101, 128, 227, 240, 241, 242, 243, 248-252, 260, 261
Closets 56, 208, 242, 244, 245, 248, 249, 263, 270
Diagrams 267, 269
Low platform 240-243, 263
Mechanisms 81, 228, 233, 258, 262-265
Power extensions 251, 252, 260
Stone 216, 257, 258, 259
Timber 40, 100, 105, 160, 170, 175, 190, 194, 208, 226, 238, 244-247, 262, 264, 270, 309

Signals
Auxiliary 128, 142, 228, 229, 231, 234, 237, 239, 290, 305
Banner repeaters 43, 45, 59, 226
Brackets 1, 26, 33, 37, 100, 128, 132, 142, 143, 149, 150, 228-239, 245, 250, 256, 261, 281, 290, 304, 310
Colour-lights 150, 161, 225, 226, 229
Fogman's huts 132, 219, 231, 248
Gantries 235, 237, 238, 239
Ground 8, 58, 68, 96, 100, 109, 227, 238, 245, 306
Guard rails 28, 219
Posts, girder 143, 232
Posts, lattice 1, 40, 73, 221, 223, 224, 228, 237, 245, 309
Posts, rail-built 44, 83, 96, 168, 219, 222, 238, 243, 273, 304
Posts, tubular 13, 60, 92, 100, 108, 142, 144, 225-228, 232, 233, 248, 310
Posts, wooden 13, 28, 34, 124, 128, 139, 160, 214-218, 230, 231, 234, 235, 236, 245, 277, 305
Sighting shields 28, 87, 142, 173, 224
Track circuit diamonds 142, 233, 248
Underslung 235, 236

Station buildings
Booking offices 21-24
Forecourts 5, 7, 8, 10, 11, 12, 15, 16, 38
Ornate 8-16, 24, 30, 36, 37, 38, 53, 60, 73, 97
Stone 8-11, 13-15, 17, 24, 34
Tiled 16, 36
Transverse (over tracks) 162, 168, 207
Waiting rooms 21, 22, 23, 85, 88, 99
Wooden 13, 21, 22, 40, 75, 86, 87, 286, 287

Station types
Closed 17, 32, 36, 80, 85-89, 97, 103, 104, 106, 286
Halts 6, 21, 49, 51, 7679, 82, 88
Overall roofs 2, 32, 103, 106, 110, 157, 159
Single-line 6, 20, 25, 39, 72, 86, 88, 93, 195, 200
Staggered platforms 14, 61, 92, 99, 101
Termini 32, 68-71, 80, 86, 159
Three or more lines 26, 27, 30, 45, 56, 85, 96, 143, 198, 237, 238, 239, 281, 306

Trackwork
Buffer stops 107, 230, 246, 274, 301, 302
Catch-points/traps 8, 14, 83, 245

Grassy 36, 43, 85, 107, 111, 127, 205-208, 282, 286
Ground frames 188, 190, 267, 268
Level crossings 6, 13, 19, 23, 40, 60, 74, 79, 92, 133, 160, 192-195, 246, 256, 282, 292
Narrow-gauge 22, 25, 70, 80, 133, 146, 180, 205, 282, 292, 293, 305
Overhead electrification (OHE) 97, 126, 275, 298, 300
Platelayers' huts 32, 73, 126, 170, 172, 218, 223, 227, 300
Point detail 34, 68, 81-84, 99-102, 106, 148, 154, 216, 218, 230, 238, 251, 254, 255, 256
Point levers 96, 109, 188-191, 212, 230, 265, 292, 293, 300, 306
Sleeper crossings 44, 79, 100, 101, 193, 198, 221, 249, 266, 308, 309

Yards
Carriage sidings 113, 161, 254
Coal sidings 84, 100, 117
Cobble stones 103, 110
Cranes 11, 107, 110, 152, 291
Debris 17, 143, 201, 270, 288, 312
Goods offices 99, 100, 101, 288
Goods stations 103-106, 110, 128
Goods yards 8, 22, 71, 82, 84, 85, 88, 89, 99-106, 128, 153, 154, 218, 227, 230, 234, 266, 281, 282
Lamps 54, 96, 100, 113, 114, 250, 290, 294, 298, 299, 300
Loading gauges 108, 109, 304
Loading platforms 43, 104, 257
Marshalling yards 111-114, 128, 154
Pens 54, 72, 102, 257
Sheds, brick 8, 71, 89, 101, 102, 104, 107, 128, 288
Sheds, stone 25, 84, 100
Sheds, timber 99, 266
Sleeper stacks 3, 113, 138, 223, 236, 246, 294, 302
Warehouses 103, 151

313 A farewell to steam in 1964 as four GWR locomotives head west through **Stroud** to a scrap yard. All are cold except for the lead GWR 'Hall' class 4-6-0, No. 6944 *Fledborough Hall*. The low tender belongs to a GWR 4700 class 2-8-0 which was introduced in 1919 for heavy freight.